MW01027729

# PATRIOTIC POETRY

## 69 GREAT AMERICAN POEMS THAT INSPIRED FREEDOM

CHRISTOPHER COLE

# INTRODUCTION

"Stories have to be told or they die, and when they die, we can't remember who we are or why we're here." – Sue Monk Kidd, author

In this collection, you'll find stories conveyed through poetry and song. Some of them will no doubt be familiar to you – like Francis Scott Key's "Star Spangled Banner" and Julia Ward Howe's "Battle Hymn of the Republic" (although many people are only familiar with the first verse). Other poems will be entirely new to you. My hope is that you'll embrace both the familiar and the unfamiliar as pieces of the American story that deserve to be remembered.

In a digital age largely driven by images and sound bytes, we've become accustomed to skimming or speed-reading, focusing long enough on the bullet points and bolded text to get the gist of what's being said. Many people are finding less time to read slowly and carefully, less motivation to digest every word of a text. And yet, this is precisely how poetry is meant to be read.

My hope is that you'll approach this book with the intention to read slowly and carefully. I believe these works are among those Francis Bacon was referring to when he said, "Some books are to be tasted, others to be swallowed, and some few to be chewed and digested . . . to be read wholly, and with diligence and attention."

I hope you'll read these works with diligence and attention. Read not merely for elegant prose and sublime poetry (although you'll certainly find the sublime here). Rather, read each of these poems as fragments that, when pieced together, reveal a part of the American story.

Be aware that not every piece of a story is elegantly written. Some of these songs and poems were written by people who were largely uneducated but who found themselves on the frontlines of history and felt compelled to document it. They felt what they were witnessing was significant enough to pass on to us.

As Sue Monk Kidd states in the epitaph above, "Stories have to be told or they die, and when they die, we can't remember who we are or why we're here." I encourage you to view this collection of poetry as a way to remember who we are and why we're here.

As you read Walt Whitman's "O Captain, My Captain," I hope you remember the grief and shock that followed the death of Abraham Lincoln.

As you read "Battle Hymn of the Republic," I hope you remember the mark left by Julia Ward Howe on the storytelling surrounding the Civil War, and how she transformed the tune to "John Brown's Body" into the version of the song we know today.

As you read Philip Freneau's "To the Memory of the Americans who Fell at Eutaw," I hope you remember the ordinary men and women who defended ordinary towns and shaped the course of American history with their stalwart heroism.

Most of all, I hope you walk away from this volume with gratitude for those who have come before us and the values and sacrifices that have shaped America's story.

My sincerest thanks,
   Christopher

# PAUL REVERE'S RIDE

## HENRY WADSWORTH LONGFELLOW

April 18th, 1775

This poem is the "Landlord's Tale," the first of the "Tales of a Wayside Inn."

\* \* \*

LISTEN, my children, and you shall hear
Of the midnight ride of Paul Revere,
On the eighteenth of April, in Seventy-five:
Hardly a man is now alive
Who remembers that famous day and year.

He said to his friend, "If the British march
By land or sea from the town to-night,
Hang a lantern aloft in the belfry arch
Of the North Church tower as a signal-light,
One, if by land, and two, if by sea;
And I on the opposite shore will be,
Ready to ride and spread the alarm
Through every Middlesex village and farm,
For the country folk to be up and to arm."

Then he said, Good-night! and with muffled oar
Silently rowed to the Charlestown shore,
Just as the moon rose over the bay,
Where swinging wide at her moorings lay
The Somerset, British man-of-war;

A phantom ship, with each mast and spar
Across the moon like a prison-bar,
And a huge black hulk, that was magnified
By its own reflection in the tide.

Meanwhile, his friend, through alley and street
Wanders and watches with eager ears,
Till in the silence around him he hears
The muster of men at the barrack door,
The sound of arms, and the tramp of feet,
And the measured tread of the grenadiers,
Marching down to their boats on the shore.

Then he climbed to the tower of the Old North Church
By the wooden stairs, with stealthy tread,
To the belfry-chamber overhead,
And startled the pigeons from their perch
On the sombre rafters, that round him made
Masses and moving shapes of shade,
By the trembling ladder, steep and tall,
To the highest window in the wall,
Where he paused to listen and look down
A moment on the roofs of the town,
And the moonlight flowing over all.

Beneath, in the churchyard, lay the dead,
In their night-encampment on the hill,
Wrapped in silence so deep and still
That he could hear, like a sentinel's tread,

The watchful night-wind, as it went
Creeping along from tent to tent,
And seeming to whisper, "All is well!"
A moment only he feels the spell
Of the place and the hour, and the secret dread
Of the lonely belfry and the dead;
For suddenly all his thoughts are bent
On a shadowy something far away,
Where the river widens to meet the bay,
A line of black that bends and floats
On the rising tide, like a bridge of boats.

Meanwhile, impatient to mount and ride,
Booted and spurred, with a heavy stride
On the opposite shore walked Paul Revere.
Now he patted his horse's side,
Now gazed at the landscape far and near,
Then, impetuous, stamped the earth,
And turned and tightened his saddle-girth;
But mostly he watched with eager search
The belfry-tower of the Old North Church,
As it rose above the graves on the hill,
Lonely, and spectral, and sombre and still.
And lo! as he looks, on the belfry's height
A glimmer, and then a gleam of light!
He springs to the saddle, the bridle he turns,
But lingers and gazes, till full on his sight
A second lamp in the belfry burns!

A hurry of hoofs in a village street,
A shape in the moonlight, a bulk in the dark,
And beneath, from the pebbles, in passing, a spark
Struck out by a steed flying fearless and fleet:
That was all! And yet, through the gloom and the light,
The fate of a nation was riding that night;
And the spark struck out by that steed, in his flight,

Kindled the land into flame with its heat.

He has left the village and mounted the steep,
And beneath him, tranquil and broad and deep,
Is the Mystic, meeting the ocean tides;
And under the alders, that skirt its edge,
Now soft on the sand, now loud on the ledge,
Is heard the tramp of his steed as he rides.

It was twelve by the village clock
When he crossed the bridge into Medford town.
He heard the crowing of the cock,
And the barking of the farmer's dog,
And felt the damp of the river fog,
That rises after the sun goes down.

It was one by the village clock,
When he rode into Lexington.
He saw the gilded weathercock
Swim in the moonlight as he passed,
And the meeting-house windows, blank and bare,
Gaze at him with a spectral glare,

As if they already stood aghast
At the bloody work they would look upon.

It was two by the village clock,
When he came to the bridge in Concord town.
He heard the bleating of the flock,
And the twitter of birds among the trees,
And felt the breath of the morning breeze
Blowing over the meadows brown.
And one was safe and asleep in his bed
Who at the bridge would be first to fall,
Who that day would be lying dead,
Pierced by a British musket-ball.

You know the rest. In the books you have read,
How the British Regulars fired and fled,
How the farmers gave them ball for ball,
From behind each fence and farm-yard wall,
Chasing the red-coats down the lane,
Then crossing the fields to emerge again
Under the trees at the turn of the road,
And only pausing to fire and load.

So through the night rode Paul Revere;
And so through the night went his cry of alarm
To every Middlesex village and farm,
A cry of defiance and not of fear,
A voice in the darkness, a knock at the door,
And a word that shall echo forevermore!

For, borne on the night-wind of the Past,
Through all our history, to the last,
In the hour of darkness and peril and need,
The people will waken and listen to hear
The hurrying hoof-beats of that steed,
And the midnight message of Paul Revere.

# JOHN BURNS OF GETTYSBURG

## BRET HAUTE

July 1st - 3rd, 1863

\* \* \*

HAVE you heard the story that gossips tell
Of Burns of Gettysburg? No? Ah, well,
Brief is the glory that hero earns,
Briefer the story of poor John Burns:
He was the fellow who won renown,
The only man who didn't back down
When the rebels rode through his native town;
But held his own in the fight next day,
When all his townsfolk ran away.
That was in July, Sixty-three,
The very day that General Lee,
Flower of Southern chivalry,
Baffled and beaten, backward reeled
From a stubborn Meade and a barren field.
I might tell how but the day before
John Burns stood at his cottage door,
Looking down the village street,
Where, in the shade of his peaceful vine,

He heard the low of his gathered kine,
And felt their breath with incense sweet
Or I might say, when the sunset burned
The old farm gable, he thought it turned

The milk that fell like a babbling flood
Into the milk-pail red as blood!
Or how he fancied the hum of bees
Were bullets buzzing among the trees.
But all such fanciful thoughts as these
Were strange to a practical man like Burns,
Who minded only his own concerns,
Troubled no more by fancies fine
Than one of his calm-eyed, long-tailed kine,
Quite old-fashioned and matter-of-fact,
Slow to argue, but quick to act.
That was the reason, as some folks say,
He fought so well on that terrible day.

And it was terrible. On the right
Raged for hours the heady fight,
Thundered the battery's double bass,
Difficult music for men to face;
While on the left where now the graves
Undulate like the living waves
That all that day unceasing swept
Up to the pits the Rebels kept
Round shot ploughed the upland glades,
Sown with bullets, reaped with blades;
Shattered fences here and there
Tossed their splinters in the air;
The very trees were stripped and bare;
The barns that once held yellow grain
Were heaped with harvests of the slain;
The cattle bellowed on the plain,
The turkeys screamed with might and main,

And brooding barn-fowl left their rest
With strange shells bursting in each nest.

Just where the tide of battle turns,
Erect and lonely stood old John Burns.
How do you think the man was dressed?
He wore an ancient long buff vest,
Yellow as saffron, but his best,
And, buttoned over his manly breast,
Was a bright blue coat, with a rolling collar,
And large gilt buttons, size of a dollar,
With tails that the country-folk called swaller.
He wore a broad-brimmed, bell-crowned hat,
White as the locks on which it sat.
Never had such a sight been seen
For forty years on the village green,
Since old John Burns was a country beau,
And went to the "quiltings" long ago.

Close at his elbows all that day,
Veterans of the Peninsula,
Sunburnt and bearded, charged away;
And striplings, downy of lip and chin,
Clerks that the Home Guard mustered in,
Glanced, as they passed, at the hat he wore,
Then at the rifle his right hand bore;
And hailed him, from out their youthful lore,

With scraps of a slangy repertoire:
"How are you, White Hat?" "Put her through!"
"Your head's level!" and "Bully for you!"
Called him "Daddy," begged he'd disclose
The name of the tailor who made his clothes,
And what was the value he set on those;
While Burns, unmindful of jeer and scoff,
Stood there picking the rebels off,-

With his long brown rifle and bell-crown hat,
And the swallow-tails they were laughing at.

'Twas but a moment, for that respect
Which clothes all courage their voices checked:
And something the wildest could understand
Spake in the old man's strong right hand,
And his corded throat, and the lurking frown
Of his eyebrows under his old bell-crown:
Until, as they gazed, there crept an awe
Through the ranks in whispers, and some men saw,
In the antique vestments and long white hair,
The Past of the Nation in battle there;
And some of the soldiers since declare
That the gleam of his old white hat afar,
Like the crested plume of the brave Navarre,
That day was their oriflamme of war.

So raged the battle. You know the rest:
How the rebels, beaten and backward pressed,
Broke at the final charge, and ran.
At which John Burns a practical man
Shouldered his rifle, unbent his brows,
And then went back to his bees and cows.

That is the story of old John Burns;
This is the moral the reader learns:
In fighting the battle, the question's whether
You'll show a hat that's white, or a feather!

# 3

# BOSTON

## RALPH WALDO EMERSON

SICUT PATRIBUS, SIT DEUS NOBIS

December 16th, 1773

This poem was read in Faneuil Hall,
on the Centennial Anniversary of the
"Boston Tea-Party" at which a
band of men disguised as Indians
had quietly emptied into the sea
the taxed tea-chests of three British ships.

\* \* \*

THE rocky nook with hill-tops three
Looked eastward from the farms,
And twice each day the flowing sea
Took Boston in its arms;
The men of yore were stout and poor,
And sailed for bread to every shore.

And where they went on trade intent
They did what freemen can,

Their dauntless ways did all men praise,
The merchant was a man.
The world was made for honest trade,
To plant and eat be none afraid.

The waves that rocked them on the deep
To them their secret told;
Said the winds that sung the lads to sleep,
"Like us be free and bold!"
The honest waves refuse to slaves
The empire of the ocean caves.

Old Europe groans with palaces,
Has lords enough and more;-
We plant and build by foaming seas
A city of the poor;
For day by day could Boston Bay
Their honest labor overpay.

We grant no dukedoms to the few,
We hold like rights and shall;
Equal on Sunday in the pew,
On Monday in the mall.
For what avail the plough or sail,
Or land or life, if freedom fail?

The noble craftsmen we promote,
Disown the knave and fool;
Each honest man shall have his vote,
Each child shall have his school.
A union then of honest men,
Or union nevermore again.

The wild rose and the barberry thorn
Hung out their summer pride
Where now on heated pavements worn

The feet of millions stride.
Fair rose the planted hills behind
The good town on the bay,
And where the western hills declined
The prairie stretched away.

What care though rival cities soar
Along the stormy coast:
Penn's town, New York, and Baltimore,
If Boston knew the most!

They laughed to know the world so wide;
The mountains said: "Good-day!
We greet you well, you Saxon men,
Up with your towns and stay!"
The world was made for honest trade,
To plant and eat be none afraid.

"For you," they said, "no barriers be,
For you no sluggard rest;
Each street leads downward to the sea,
Or landward to the West."

O happy town beside the sea,
Whose roads lead everywhere to all;
Than thine no deeper moat can be,
No stouter fence, no steeper wall!

Bad news from George on the English throne:
"You are thriving well," said he;
"Now by these presents be it known,
You shall pay us a tax on tea;
'Tis very small, no load at all,
Honor enough that we send the call."

"Not so," said Boston, "good my lord,

We pay your governors here
Abundant for their bed and board,
Six thousand pounds a year.
(Your highness knows our homely word,)
Millions for self-government,
But for tribute never a cent."

The cargo came! and who could blame
If Indians seized the tea,
And, chest by chest, let down the same
Into the laughing sea?
For what avail the plough or sail
Or land or life, if freedom fail?

The townsmen braved the English king,
Found friendship in the French,
And Honor joined the patriot ring
Low on their wooden bench.

O bounteous seas that never fail!
O day remembered yet!
O happy port that spied the sail
Which wafted Lafayette!

Pole-star of light in Europe's night,
That never faltered from the right.

Kings shook with fear, old empires crave
The secret force to find
Which fired the little State to save
The rights of all mankind.

But right is might through all the world;
Province to province faithful clung,
Through good and ill the war-bolt hurled,
Till Freedom cheered and the joy-bells rung.

The sea returning day by day
Restores the world-wide mart;
So let each dweller on the Bay
Fold Boston in his heart,
Till these echoes be choked with snows,
Or over the town blue ocean flows.

Let the blood of her hundred thousands
Throb in each manly vein;
And the wit of all her wisest
Make sunshine in her brain.
For you can teach the lightning speech,
And round the globe your voices reach.

And each shall care for other,
And each to each shall bend,
To the poor a noble brother,
To the good an equal friend.

A blessing through the ages thus
Shield all thy roofs and towers!
God with the fathers, so with us,
Thou darling town of ours!

# 4

# KEENAN'S CHARGE

## GEORGE PARSONS LATHROP

May 2nd, 1863

During the second day of the battle of Chancellorsville, General
Pleasonton was trying to get twenty-two guns into a vital
position as Stonewall Jackson made a sudden advance. Time had
to be bought; so Pleasonton ordered Major Peter Keenan,
commanding the Eighth Pennsylvania Cavalry (four hundred
strong), to charge the advancing ten thousand of the enemy. An
introduction to the poem, setting forth these facts, is omitted.

\* \* \*

BY the shrouded gleam of the western skies,
Brave Keenan looked in Pleasonton's eyes
For an instant clear, and cool, and still;
Then, with a smile, he said: "I will."

"Cavalry, charge!" Not a man of them shrank.
Their sharp, full cheer, from rank on rank,
Rose joyously, with a willing breath-
Rose like a greeting hail to death.
Then forward they sprang, and spurred and clashed;

Shouted the officers, crimson-sash'd;
Rode well the men, each brave as his fellow,
In their faded coats of the blue and yellow;
And above in the air, with an instinct true,
Like a bird of war their pennon flew.

With clank of scabbards and thunder of steeds,
And blades that shine like sunlit reeds,
And strong brown faces bravely pale
For fear their proud attempt shall fail,
Three hundred Pennsylvanians close
On twice ten thousand gallant foes.

Line after line the troopers came
To the edge of the wood that was ring'd with flame;
Rode in and sabred and shot and fell;
Nor came one back his wounds to tell.
And full in the midst rose Keenan, tall
In the gloom, like a martyr awaiting his fall,
While the circle-stroke of his sabre, swung
'Round his head, like a halo there, luminous hung.

Line after line; ay, whole platoons,
Struck dead in their saddles, of brave dragoons
By the maddened horses were onward borne
And into the vortex flung, trampled and torn;
As Keenan fought with his men, side by side.

So they rode, till there were no more to ride.

But over them, lying there, shattered and mute,
What deep echo rolls?- 'Tis a death salute
From the cannon in place; for, heroes, you braved
Your fate not in vain: the army was saved!

Over them now year following year

Over their graves, the pine-cones fall,
And the whip-poor-will chants his spectre-call;
But they stir not again: they raise no cheer:
They have ceased. But their glory shall never cease,
Nor their light be quenched in the light of peace.
The rush of their charge is resounding still
That saved the army at Chancellorsville.

# 5

# THE BATTLE OF LEXINGTON

## SIDNEY LANIER

April 19th, 1775

The skirmish at Lexington and the fight at Concord closed all political bickering between Great Britain and her colonies and began the War of the Revolution. The following verses are a fragment of the "Psalm of the West."

THEN haste ye, Prescott and Revere!
Bring all the men of Lincoln here;
Let Chelmsford, Littleton, Carlisle,
Let Acton, Bedford, hither file
On, hither file, and plainly see
Out of a wound leap Liberty.

Say, Woodman April! all in green,
Say, Robin April! hast thou seen
In all thy travel round the earth
Ever a morn of calmer birth?
But Morning's eye alone serene
Can gaze across yon village-green

To where the trooping British run
Through Lexington.
Good men in fustian, stand ye still;
The men in red come o'er the hill,
Lay down your arms, damned rebels! cry
The men in red full haughtily.
But never a grounding gun is heard;

The men in fustian stand unstirred;
Dead calm, save maybe a wise bluebird
Puts in his little heavenly word.
O men in red! if ye but knew
The half as much as bluebirds do,
Now in this little tender calm
Each hand would out, and every palm
With patriot palm strike brotherhood's stroke
Or ere these lines of battle broke.

O men in red! if ye but knew
The least of all that bluebirds do,
Now in this little godly cairn
Yon voice might sing the Future's Psalm
The Psalm of Love with the brotherly eyes
Who pardons and is very wise
Yon voice that shouts, high-hoarse with ire,
Fire!

The red-coats fire, the homespuns fall:
The homespuns' anxious voices call,
Brother, art hurt? and Where hit, John?
And, Wipe this blood., and Men, come on,
And Neighbor, do but lift my head,
And Who is wounded? Who is dead?
Seven are killed. My God! my God!
Seven lie dead on the village sod.
Two Harringtons, Parker, Hadley, Brown,

Monroe and Porter, these are down.

Nay, look! stout Harrington not yet dead.
He crooks his elbow, lifts his head.
He lies at the step of his own house-door;
He crawls and makes a path of gore.
The wife from the window hath seen, and rushed;
He hath reached the step, but the blood hath gushed;
He hath crawled to the step of his own house-door,
But his head hath dropped: he will crawl no more.
Clasp Wife, and kiss, and lift the head,
Harrington lies at his doorstep dead.

But, O ye Six that round him lay
And bloodied up that April day!
As Harrington fell, ye likewise fell
At the door of the House wherein ye dwell;
As Harrington came, ye likewise came
And died at the door of your House of Fame.

# 6

# MUSIC IN CAMP

## JOHN R. THOMPSON

December 15th - 31st, 1862

\* \* \*

TWO armies covered hill and plain
Where Rappahannock's waters
Ran deeply crimsoned with the stain
Of battle's recent slaughters.

The summer clouds lay pitched like tents
In meads of heavenly azure;
And each dread gun of the elements
Slept in its hid embrasure.

The breeze so softly blew, it made
No forest leaf to quiver,
And the smoke of the random cannonade
Rolled slowly from the river.

And now where circling hills looked down
With cannon grimly planted,

O'er listless camp and silent town
The golden sunset slanted;

When on the fervid air there came
A strain, now rich, now tender,
The music seemed itself aflame
With day's departing splendor.

A Federal band, which eve and morn
Played measures brave and nimble,
Had just struck up with flute and horn
And lively clash of cymbal.

Down flocked the soldiers to the bank;
Till margined by its pebbles,
One wooded shore was blue with 'Yanks,
And one was gray with "Rebels."

Then all was still; and then the band
With movements light and tricksy,
Made stream and forest, hill and strand,
Reverberate with "Dixie."

The conscious stream, with burnished glow,
Went proudly o'er its pebbles,
But thrilled throughout its deepest flow
With yelling of the Rebels.

Again a pause, and then again
The trumpet pealed sonorous,
And Yankee Doodle was the strain
To which the shore gave chorus.

The laughing ripple shoreward flew
To kiss the shining pebbles

Loud shrieked the crowding Boys in Blue
Defiance to the Rebels.

And yet once more the bugle sang
Above the stormy riot;
No shout upon the evening rang
There reigned a holy quiet.

The sad, lone stream its noiseless tread
Spread o'er the glistening pebbles:
All silent now the Yankees stood;
All silent stood the Rebels:

For each responsive soul had heard
That plaintive note's appealing,
So deeply "Home, Sweet Home" had stirred
The hidden founts of feeling.

Or blue or gray, the soldier sees,
As by the wand of fairy,
The cottage neath the live-oak trees,
The cottage by the prairie.

Or cold or warm, his native skies
Bend in their beauty o'er him:
Sending the tear-mist in his eyes
The dear ones stand before him.

As fades the iris after rain
In April's tearful weather,
The vision vanished as the strain
And daylight died together.

But memory, waked by music's art
Expressed in simplest numbers,

Subdued the sternest Yankee's heart,
Made light the Rebel's slumbers.

And fair the form of Music shines,
That bright, celestial creature,
Who still 'mid war's embattled lines
Gave this one touch of nature.

# HYMN

## RALPH WALDO EMERSON

April 19th, 1775

This poem was written to be sung at the completion of
the Concord Monument, April 19, 1836

\* \* \*

BY the rude bridge that arched the flood,
Their flag to April's breeze unfurled,
Here once the embattled farmers stood,
And fired the shot heard round the world.

The foe long since in silence slept;
Alike the conqueror silent sleeps;
And Time the ruined bridge has swept
Down the dark stream which seaward creeps.

On this green bank, by this soft stream,
We set to-day a votive stone;
That memory may their deed redeem,
When, like our sires, our sons are gone.

Spirit, that made those heroes dare
To die, or leave their children free,
Bid Time and Nature gently spare
The shaft we raise to them and thee.

# FREDERICKSBURG

## THOMAS BAILEY ALDRICH

December 13th, 1862

\* \* \*

THE increasing moonlight drifts across my bed,
And on the churchyard by the road, I know
It falls as white and noiselessly as snow.
'Twas such a night two weary summers fled;
The stars, as now, were waning overhead.
Listen! Again the shrill-lipped bugles blow
Where the swift currents of the river flow
Past Fredericksburg: far off the heavens are red
With sudden conflagration: on yon height,
Linstock in hand, the gunners hold their breath:
A signal-rocket pierces the dense night,
Flings its spent stars upon the town beneath:
Hark! the artillery massing on the right,
Hark! the black squadrons wheeling down to Death!

# TICONDEROGA

## V. B. WILSON

May 10th, 1775

After the news of Concord fight,
a volunteer expedition
from Vermont and Connecticut,
under Ethan Allen and
Benedict Arnold,
seized Ticonderoga and Crown Point,
whose military stores were of great service.
From its chime of bells,
the French called Ticonderoga "Carillon."

\* \* \*

THE cold, gray light of the dawning
On old Carillon falls,
And dim in the mist of the morning
Stand the grim old fortress walls.
No sound disturbs the stillness
Save the cataract's mellow roar,
Silent as death is the fortress,
Silent the misty shore.

But up from the wakening waters
Comes the cool, fresh morning breeze,
Lifting the banner of Britain,
And whispering to the trees
Of the swift gliding boats on the waters
That are nearing the fog-shrouded land,
With the old Green Mountain Lion,
And his daring patriot band.

But the sentinel at the postern
Heard not the whisper low;
He is dreaming of the banks of the Shannon
As he walks on his beat to and fro,
Of the starry eyes in Green Erin
That were dim when he marched away,
And a tear down his bronzed cheek courses,
'Tis the first for many a day.

A sound breaks the misty stillness,
And quickly he glances around;
Through the mist, forms like towering giants
Seem rising out of the ground;
A challenge, the firelock flashes,
A sword cleaves the quivering air,
And the sentry lies dead by the postern,
Blood staining his bright yellow hair.

Then, with a shout that awakens
All the echoes of hillside and glen,
Through the low, frowning gate of the fortress,
Sword in hand, rush the Green Mountain men.
The scarce wakened troops of the garrison
Yield up their trust pale with fear;
And down comes the bright British banner,
And out rings a Green Mountain cheer.

Flushed with pride, the whole eastern heavens
With crimson and gold are ablaze;

And up springs the sun in his splendor
And flings down his arrowy rays,
Bathing in sunlight the fortress,
Turning to gold the grim walls,
While louder and clearer and higher
Rings the song of the waterfalls.

Since the taking of Ticonderoga
A century has rolled away;
But with pride the nation remembers
That glorious morning in May.
And the cataract's silvery music
Forever the story tells,
Of the capture of old Carillon,
The chime of the silver bells.

# THE BLACK REGIMENT

## GEORGE H. BOKER

May 27th, 1863

"The colored troops fought nobly" was a frequent phrase in war bulletins; never did they better deserve this praise than at Port Hudson.

\* \* \*

DARK as the clouds of even.
Ranked in the western heaven,
Waiting the breath that lifts
All the dread mass, and drifts
Tempest and falling brand
Over a ruined land;
So still and orderly,
Arm to arm, knee to knee,
Waiting the great event,
Stands the black regiment.

Down the long dusky line
Teeth gleam and eyeballs shine;
And the bright bayonet,

Bristling and firmly set,
Flashed with a purpose grand,
Long ere the sharp command
Of the fierce rolling drum
Told them their time had come,
Told them what work was sent
For the black regiment.

"Now," the flag-sergeant cried,
'Though death and hell betide,
Let the whole nation see
If we are fit to be
Free in this land; or bound
Down, like the whining hound,

Bound with red stripes of pain
In our old chains again!
O, what a shout there went
From the black regiment!

"Charge!" Trump and drum awoke,
Onward the bondmen broke;
Bayonet and sabre-stroke
Vainly opposed their rush.
Through the wild battle's crush.
With but one thought aflush,
Driving their lords like chaff,
In the guns' mouths they laugh;
Or at the slippery brands
Leaping with open hands,
Down they tear man and horse,
Down in their awful course;
Trampling with bloody heel
Over the crashing steel,
All their eyes forward bent,
Rushed the black regiment.

"Freedom!" their battle-cry,
"Freedom! or leave to die!"
Ah! and they meant the word,
Not as with us 'tis heard,
Not a mere party shout:
They gave their spirits out;
Trusted the end to God,
And on the gory sod
Rolled in triumphant blood.

Glad to strike one free blow,
Whether for weal or woe;
Glad to breathe one free breath,
Though on the lips of death.
Praying alas! in vain!
That they might fall again,
So they could once more see
That burst to liberty!
This was what "freedom" lent
To the black regiment.

Hundreds on hundreds fell;
But they are resting well;
Scourges and shackles strong
Never shall do them wrong.
O, to the living few,
Soldiers, be just and true!
Hail them as comrades tried;
Fight with them side by side;
Never, in field or tent,
Scorn the black regiment.

# WARREN'S ADDRESS

## JOHN PIERPONT

June 17th, 1775

Joseph Warren was commissioned by Massachusetts as a Major-General three days before the battle of Bunker Hill, at which he fought as a volunteer. He was one of the last to leave the field, and as a British officer in the redoubt called to him to surrender, a ball struck him in the forehead, killing him instantly.

STAND! the ground's your own. my braves!
Will ye give it up to slaves?
Will ye look for greener graves?
Hope ye mercy still?
What's the mercy despots feel?
Hear it in that battle-peal!
Read it on yon bristling steel.
Ask it, ye who will.

Fear ye foes who kill for hire?
Will ye to your homes retire?
Look behind you! they're a-fire!

And, before you, see
Who have done it! From the vale
On they come! And will ye quail?
Leaden rain and iron hail
Let their welcome be!

In the God of battles trust!
Die we may, and die we must;
But, O, where can dust to dust
Be consigned so well,
As where Heaven its dews shall shed
On the martyred patriot's bed,
And the rocks shall raise their head,
Of his deeds to tell!

# BARBARA FRIETCHIE

## JOHN GREENLEAF WHITTIER

September 6th, 1862

These lines were suggested by a newspaper paragraph which lacked foundation in fact.

\* \* \*

UP from the meadows rich with corn,
Clear in the cool September morn.

The clustered spires of Frederick stand
Green-walled by the hills of Maryland.

Round about them orchards sweep,
Apple and peach tree fruited deep,

Fair as a garden of the Lord
To the eyes of the famished rebel horde,

On that pleasant morn of the early fall,
When Lee marched over the mountain-wall,-

Over the mountains winding down,
Horse and foot, into Frederick town.

Forty flags with their silver stars,
Forty flags with their crimson bars,

Flapped in the morning wind: the sun
Of noon looked down, and saw not one.

Up rose old Barbara Frietchie then,
Bowed with her fourscore years and ten;

Bravest of all in Frederick town,
She took up the flag the men hauled down;

In her attic window the staff she set,
To show that one heart was loyal yet.

Up the street came the rebel tread,
Stonewall Jackson riding ahead.

Under his slouched hat left and right
He glanced; the old flag met his sight.

"Halt!" -the dust-brown ranks stood fast.
"Fire!" out blazed the rifle-blast.

It shivered the window, pane and sash;
It rent the banner with seam and gash.

Quick, as it fell, from the broken staff
Dame Barbara snatched the silken scarf;

She leaned far out on the window-sill,
And shook it forth with a royal will.

"Shoot, if you must, this old gray head,
But spare your country's flag," she said.

A shade of sadness, a blush of shame,
Over the face of the leader came;

The nobler nature within him stirred
To life at that woman's deed and word:

Who touches a hair of yon gray head
Dies like a dog! March on! he said.

All day long through Frederick street
Sounded the tread of marching feet:

All day long that free flag tost
Over the heads of the rebel host.

Ever its torn folds rose and fell
On the loyal winds that loved it well;

And through the hill-gaps sunset light
Shone over it with a warm good-night.

Barbara Frietchie's work is o'er,
And the Rebel rides on his raids no more.

Honor to her! and let a tear
Fall, for her sake, on Stonewall's bier.

Over Barbara Frietchie's grave,
Flag of Freedom and Union, wave!

Peace and order and beauty draw
Round thy symbol of light and law;

And ever the stars above look down
On thy stars below in Frederick town!

# GRANDMOTHER'S STORY OF BUNKER HILL BATTLE

## OLIVER WENDELL HOLMES

June 17th, 1775

### AS SHE SAW IT FROM THE BELFRY

\* \* \*

TIS like stirring living embers when, at eighty, one
    remembers.
All the achings and the quakings of "the times that tried
    men's souls";
When I talk of Whig and Tory, when I tell the Rebel story,
To you the words are ashes, but to me they're burning
    coals.

I had heard the muskets' rattle of the April running battle;
Lord Percy's hunted soldiers, I can see their red coats
    still;
But a deadly chill comes o'er me, as the day looms up
    before me.
When a thousand men lay bleeding on the slopes of
    Bunker's Hill.

'Twas a peaceful summer's morning, when the first thing
    gave us warning,
Was the booming of the cannon from the river and the
    shore:
"Child," says grandma, "what's the matter, what is all this
    noise and clatter?
Have those scalping Indian devils come to murder us
    once more?"

Poor old soul! My sides were shaking in the midst of all
    my quaking.
To hear her talk of Indians when the guns began to roar:
She had seen the burning village, and the slaughter and
    the pillage,
When the Mohawks killed her father, with their bullets
    through his door.

Then I said, "Now, dear old granny, don't you fret and
    worry any,
For I'll soon come back and tell you whether this is work
    or play;
There can't be mischief in it, so I won't be gone a minute"
For a minute then I started. I was gone the livelong day.

No time for bodice-lacing or for looking-glass grimacing;
Down my hair went as I hurried, tumbling half-way to
    my heels;
God forbid your ever knowing, when there's blood
    around her flowing,
How the lonely, helpless daughter of a quiet household
    feels!

In the street I heard a thumping; and I knew it was the
    stumping
Of the Corporal, our old neighbor, on that wooden leg he
    wore,

With a knot of women round him, it was lucky I had
 found him,
So I followed with the others, and the Corporal marched
 before.

They were making for the steeple, the old soldier and his
 people;
The pigeons circled round us as we climbed the creaking
 stair,
Just across the narrow river O, so close it made me shiver!
Stood a fortress on the hilltop that but yesterday was
 bare.

Not slow our eyes to find it; well w r e knew who stood
 behind it,
Though the earthwork hid them from us, and the
 stubborn walls were dumb:
Here were sister, wife, and mother, looking wild upon
 each other,
And their lips were white with terror as they said, THE
 HOUR HAS COME!

The morning slowly wasted, not a morsel had we tasted,
And our heads were almost splitting with the cannons'
 deafening thrill,
When a figure tall and stately round the rampart strode
 sedately;
It was PRESCOTT, one since told me; he commanded on
 the hill.

Every woman's heart grew bigger when we saw his manly
 figure,
With the banyan buckled round it, standing up so straight
 and tall;
Like a gentleman of leisure who is strolling out for
 pleasure,

Through the storm of shells and cannon-shot he walked
    around the wall.

At eleven the streets were swarming, for the red-coats'
    ranks were forming;
At noon in marching order they were moving to the
    piers;
How the bayonets gleamed and glistened, as we looked
    far down and listened
To the trampling and the drum-beat of the belted
    grenadiers!

At length the men have started, with a cheer (it seemed
    faint-hearted),
In their scarlet regimentals, with their knapsacks on their
    backs,
And the reddening, rippling water, as after a sea-fight's
    slaughter,
Round the barges gliding onward blushed like blood
    along their tracks.

So they crossed to the other border, and again they
    formed in order;
And the boats came back for soldiers, came for soldiers,
    soldiers still:
The time seemed everlasting to us women faint and
    fasting,
At last they're moving, marching, marching proudly up
    the hill.

We can see the bright steel glancing all along the lines
    advancing
Now the front rank fires a volley they have thrown away
    their shot;
For behind the earthwork lying, all the balls above them
    flying,

Our people need not hurry; so they wait and answer not.

Then the Corporal, our old cripple (he would swear
    sometimes and tipple),
He had heard the bullets whistle (in the old French war)
    be-fore,
Calls out in words of jeering, just as if they all were
    hearing,
And his wooden leg thumps fiercely on the dusty belfry
    floor:

"Oh! fire away, ye villains, and earn King George's
    shillin's,
But ye'll waste a ton of powder afore a 'rebel' falls;
You may bang the dirt and welcome, they're as safe as
    Dan'l Malcolm
Ten foot beneath the gravestone that you've splintered
    with your balls!"

In the hush of expectation, in the awe and trepidation
Of the dread approaching moment, we are well-nigh
    breathless all;
Though the rotten bars are failing on the rickety belfry
    railing,
We are crowding up against them like the waves against a
    wall.

Just a glimpse (the air is clearer), they are nearer, nearer,
    nearer,
When a flash a curling smoke-wreath then a crash the
    steeple shakes
The deadly truce is ended; the tempest's shroud is rended;
Like a morning mist it gathered, like a thunder-cloud it
    breaks!

O the sight our eyes discover as the blue-black smoke
blows over!
The red-coats stretched in windrows as a mower rakes
his hay;
Here a scarlet heap is lying, there a headlong crowd is
flying
Like a billow that has broken and is shivered into spray.

Then we cried, "The troops are routed! they are beat it
can't be doubted!
God be thanked, the fight is over!" Ah! the grim old
soldier's smile!
"Tell us, tell us why you look so?" (we could hardly speak,
we shook so),
"Are they beaten? Are they beaten? ARE they beaten?"
"Wait a while."

O the trembling and the terror! for too soon we saw our
error:
They are baffled, not defeated; we have driven them back
in vain;
And the columns that were scattered, round the colors
that were tattered,
Toward the sullen silent fortress turn their belted breasts
again.

All at once, as we are gazing, lo the roofs of Charlestown
blazing!
They have fired the harmless village; in an hour it will be
down!
The Lord in heaven confound them, rain his fire and
brimstone round them,
The robbing, murdering red-coats, that would burn a
peaceful town!

They are marching, stern and solemn; we can see each
massive column
As they near the naked earth-mound with the slanting
walls so steep.
Have our soldiers got faint-hearted, and in noiseless haste
departed?
Are they panic-struck and helpless? Are they palsied or
asleep?

Now! the walls they're almost under! scarce a rod the foes
asunder!
Not a firelock flashed against them! up the earthwork
they will swarm!
But the words have scarce been spoken, when the
ominous calm is broken,
And a bellowing crash has emptied all the vengeance of
the storm!

So again, with murderous slaughter, pelted backward to
the water,
Fly Pigot's running heroes and the frightened braves of
Howe;
And we shout, "At last they're done for, it's their barges
they have run for:
They are beaten, beaten, beaten; and the battle's over
now!"

And we looked, poor timid creatures, on the rough old
soldier's features,
Our lips afraid to question, but he knew what we
would ask:
"Not sure," he said; "keep quiet, once more, I guess, they'll
try it-
Here's damnation to the cut-throats!" then he handed me
his flask,

Saying, "Gal, you're looking shaky; have a drop of old
    Jamaiky:
I'm afraid there'll be more trouble afore this job is done;"
So I took one scorching swallow; dreadful faint I felt and
    hollow,
Standing there from early morning when the firing was
    begun.

All through those hours of trial I had watched a calm
    clock dial,
As the hands kept creeping, creeping, they were creeping
    round to four,
When the old man said, "They're forming with their
    bayonets fixed for storming:
It's the death grip that's a coming, they will try the works
    once more."

With brazen trumpets blaring, the flames behind them
    glaring,
The deadly wall before them, in close array they come;
Still onward, upward toiling, like a dragon's fold
    uncoiling
Like the rattlesnake's shrill warning the reverberating
    drum!

Over heaps all torn and gory shall I tell the fearful story,
How they surged above the breastwork, as a sea breaks
    over a deck;
How, driven, yet scarce defeated, our worn-out men
    retreated,
With their powder-horns all emptied, like the swimmers
    from a wreck?

It has all been told and painted; as for me, they say I
    fainted,

And the wooden-legged old Corporal stumped with me
　　down the stair:
When I woke from dreams affrighted the evening lamps
　　were lighted,
On the floor a youth was lying; his bleeding breast was
　　bare.

And I heard through ail the flurry, "Send for WARREN!
　　hurry! hurry!
Tell him here's a soldier bleeding, and he'll come and
　　dress his wound!"
Ah, we knew not till the morrow told its tale of death and
　　sorrow,
How the starlight found him stiffened on the dark and
　　bloody ground.

Who the youth was, what his name was, where the place
　　from which he came was,
Who had brought him from the battle, and had left him at
　　our door,
He could not speak to tell us; but 'twas one of our brave
　　fellows,
As the homespun plainly showed us which the dying
　　soldier wore.

For they all thought he was dying, as they gathered 'round
　　him crying,
And they said, "O, how they'll miss him!" and, "What will
　　his mother do?"
Then, his eyelids just unclosing like a child's that has been
　　dozing,
He faintly murmured, "Mother!" and I saw his eyes were
　　blue.

"Why, grandma, how you're winking!" Ah, my child, it
　　sets me thinking

Of a story not like this one. Well, he somehow lived
    along;
So we came to know each other, and I nursed him like a
    mother,
Till at last he stood before me, tall, and rosy-cheeked, and
    strong.

And we sometimes walked together in the pleasant
    summer weather;
"Please to tell us what his name was?" -Just your own, my
    little dear,
There's his picture Copley painted: we became so well
    acquainted,
That in short, that's why I'm grandma, and you children
    all are here!

# KEARNY AT SEVEN PINES

## EDMUND CLARENCE STEDMAN

May 31, 1862

* * *

SO that soldierly legend is still on its journey,
That story of Kearny who knew not to yield!
'Twas the day when with Jameson, fierce Berry, and
    Birney,
Against twenty thousand he rallied the field,
Where the red volleys poured, where the clamor rose
    highest,
Where the dead lay in clumps through the dwarf oak and
    pine,
Where the aim from the thicket was surest and nighest,-
No charge like Phil Kearny's along the whole line.

When the battle went ill, and the bravest were solemn,
Near the dark Seven Pines, where we still held our
    ground,
He rode down the length of the withering column,
And his heart at our war-cry leapt up with a bound;
He snuffed, like his charger, the wind of our powder,-

His sword waved us on and we answered the sign:
Loud our cheer as we rushed, but his laugh rang the
    louder,
"There's the devil's own fun, boys, along the whole line!"

How he strode his brown steed! How we saw his blade
    brighten
In the one hand still left, and the reins in his teeth!
He laughed like a boy when the holidays heighten,
But a soldier's glance shot from his visor beneath.
Up came the reserves to the mellay infernal,
Asking where to go in, through the clearing or pine?
"O, anywhere! Forward! 'Tis all the same, Colonel:
You'll find lovely fighting along the whole line!"

O, evil the black shroud of night at Chantilly,
That hid him from sight of his brave men and tried!
Foul, foul sped the bullet that clipped the white lily,
The flower of our knighthood, the whole army's pride!
Yet we dream that he still, in that shadowy region
Where the dead form their ranks at the wan drummer's
    sign,-
Rides on, as of old, down the length of his legion,
And the word still is Forward! along the whole line.

# NATHAN HALE

## FRANCIS MILES FINCH

September 22nd, 1776

After the retreat from Long Island, Washington needed information as to the British strength. Captain Nathan Hale, a young man of twenty-one, volunteered to get this. He was taken, inside the enemy's lines, and hanged as a spy, regretting that he had but one life to lose for his country.

TO drum-beat and heart-beat,
A soldier marches by:
There is color in his cheek,
There is courage in his eye,
Yet to drum-beat and heart-beat
In a moment he must die.

By starlight and moonlight,
He seeks the Briton's camp;
He hears the rustling flag,
And the armed sentry's tramp;
And the starlight and moonlight

His silent wanderings lamp.

With slow tread and still tread,
He scans the tented line;
And he counts the battery guns
By the gaunt and shadowy pine;
And his slow tread and still tread
Gives no warning sign.

The dark wave, the plumed wave,
It meets his eager glance;
And it sparkles 'neath the stars,
Like the glimmer of a lance
A dark wave, a plumed wave,
On an emerald expanse.

A sharp clang, a steel clang,
And terror in the sound!
For the sentry, falcon-eyed,
In the camp a spy hath found;
With a sharp clang, a steel clang,
The patriot is bound.

With calm brow, steady brow,
He listens to his doom;
In his look there is no fear,
Nor a shadow-trace of gloom;
But with calm brow and steady brow
He robes him for the tomb.

In the long night, the still night,
He kneels upon the sod;
And the brutal guards withhold
E'en the solemn Word of God!
In the long night, the still night,
He walks where Christ hath trod.

'Neath the blue morn, the sunny morn,
He dies upon the tree;
And he mourns that he can lose
But one life for Liberty;
And in the blue morn, the sunny morn,
His spirit-wings are free.

But his last words, his message-words,
They burn, lest friendly eye
Should read how proud and calm
A patriot could die,
With his last words, his dying words,
A soldier's battle-cry.

From the Fame-leaf and Angel-leaf,
From monument and urn,
The sad of earth, the glad of heaven,
His tragic fate shall learn;
And on Fame-leaf and Angel-leaf
The name of HALE shall burn.

1 6

# DIRGE FOR A SOLDIER

## GEORGE H. BOKER

September 1, 1862

These verses were written in memory of General Philip Kearny,
killed at Chantilly after he had ridden out in advance of his men
to reconnoitre.

CLOSE his eyes; his work is done!
What to him is friend or foeman,
Rise of moon, or set of sun,
Hand of man, or kiss of woman?
Lay him low, lay him low,
In the clover or the snow!
What cares he? he can not know:
Lay him low!

As man may, he fought his fight,
Proved his truth by his endeavor;
Let him sleep in solemn night,
Sleep forever and forever.
Lay him low, lay him low,

In the clover or the snow!
What cares he? he can not know:
Lay him low!

Fold him in his country's stars,
Roll the drum and fire the volley!
What to him are all our wars,
What but death bemocking folly?
Lay him low, lay him low,
In the clover or the snow!
What cares he? he can not know:
Lay him low!

Leave him to God's watching eye,
Trust him to the hand that made him.
Mortal love weeps idly by:
God alone has power to aid him,
Lay him low, lay him low,
In the clover or the snow!
What cares he? he can not know:
Lay him low!

# THE OLD CONTINENTALS

## GUY HUMPHREY MCMASTER

1775 - 1783

The nucleus of the Continental Army was the New England
force gathered before Boston, to the command of which
Washington had been appointed two days before the battle of
Bunker Hill, although he arrived too late to take part in that
fight.

\* \* \*

IN their ragged regimentals
Stood the old continentals,
Yielding not,
When the grenadiers were lunging,
And like hail fell the plunging
Cannon-shot;
When the files
Of the isles
From the smoky night encampment, bore the banner of the
rampant

Unicorn,

And grummer, grummer, grummer rolled the roll of the
drummer,

Through the morn!

Then with eyes to the front all,
And with guns horizontal,
Stood our sires;

And the balls whistled deadly,
And in streams flashing redly
Blazed the fires;
As the roar
On the shore,
Swept the strong battle-breakers o'er the green-sodded acres Of
the plain;
And louder, louder, louder cracked the black gunpowder,
Cracking amain!

Now like smiths at their forges
Worked the red St. George's
Cannoneers;
And the "villainous saltpetre"
Rung a fierce, discordant metre
Round their ears;
As the swift
Storm-drift,
With hot sweeping anger, came the horse-guards' clangor On
our flanks.
Then higher, higher, higher burned the old-fashioned fire
Through the ranks!

Then the old-fashioned colonel
Galloped through the white infernal
Powder-cloud;
And his broad-sword was swinging,

And his brazen throat was ringing
Trumpet loud.
Then the blue
Bullets flew,
And the trooper-jackets redden at the touch of the leaden
Rifle-breath;
And rounder, rounder, rounder roared the iron six pounder,
Hurling death!

# 18

# THE BIVOUAC OF THE DEAD

## THEODORE O'HARA

February 22nd, 23rd, 1847

This poem was written to commemorate the bringing home of the bodies of the Kentucky soldiers who fell at Buena Vista, and their burial at Frankfort at the cost of the State.

\* \* \*

THE muffled drum's sad roll has beat
The soldier's last tattoo;
No more on life's parade shall meet
That brave and fallen few.
On fame's eternal camping ground
Their silent tents are spread,
And glory guards, with solemn round,
The bivouac of the dead.

No rumor of the foe's advance
Now swells upon the wind;
No troubled thought at midnight haunts
Of loved ones left behind;
No vision of the morrow's strife

The warrior's dream alarms;
No braying horn, nor screaming fife,
At dawn shall call to arms.

Their shivered swords are red with rust,
Their plumed heads are bowed;
Their haughty banner, trailed in dust,
Is now their martial shroud.
And plenteous funeral tears have washed
The red stains from each brow,
And the proud forms, by battle gashed,
Are free from anguish now.

The neighing troop, the flashing blade,
The bugle's stirring blast,
The charge, the dreadful cannonade,
The din and shout are past;
Nor war's wild note nor glory's peal
Shall thrill with fierce delight
Those breasts that never more may feel
The rapture of the fight.

Like the fierce northern hurricane
That sweeps his great plateau,
Flushed with the triumph yet to gain,
Came down the serried foe.
Who heard the thunder of the fray
Break o'er the field beneath,
Knew well the watchword of that day
Was "Victory or death."

Long had the doubtful conflict raged
O'er all that stricken plain,
For never fiercer fight had waged
The vengeful blood of Spain;
And still the storm of battle blew,

Still swelled the gory tide;
Not long, our stout old chieftain knew,
Such odds his strength could bide.

'Twas in that hour his stern command
Called to a martyr's grave
The flower of his beloved land,
The nation's flag to save.
By rivers of their father's gore
His first-born laurels grew,
And well he deemed the sons would pour
Their lives for glory too.

Full many a norther's breath has swept
O'er Angostura's plain
And long the pitying sky has wept
Above the mouldering slain.
The raven's scream, or eagle's flight,
Or shepherd's pensive lay,
Alone awakes each sullen height
That frowned o'er that dread fray.

Sons of the Dark and Bloody Ground,
Ye must not slumber there,
Where stranger steps and tongues resound
Along the heedless air;
Your own proud land's heroic soil
Shall be your fitter grave;
She claims from war his richest spoil
The ashes of her brave.

So, 'neath their parent turf they rest,
Far from the gory field,
Borne to a Spartan mother's breast,
On many a bloody shield;
The sunshine of their native sky

Smiles sadly on them here,
And kindred eyes and hearts watch by
The heroes' sepulchre.

Rest on, embalmed and sainted dead,
Dear as the blood ye gave;
No impious footstep here shall tread
The herbage of your grave;
Nor shall your glory be forgot
While Fame her record keeps,
Or Honor points the hallowed spot
Where Valor proudly sleeps.

Yon marble minstrel's voiceless stone,
In deathless song shall tell,
When many a vanished age hath flown
The story how ye fell;
Nor wreck, nor change, nor winter's blight,
Nor Time's remorseless doom,
Shall dim one ray of glory's light
That gilds your deathless tomb.

# 19

# THE BATTLE OF NEW ORLEANS

## THOMAS DUNN ENGLISH

January 8th, 1815

The treaty of peace between Great Britain and the United States
was signed at Ghent, December 14, 1814; but before the news
crossed the ocean, Pakenham, with twelve thousand British
veterans, attacked New Orleans, defended by Andrew Jackson
with five thousand Americans, mostly militia. The British were
repulsed with a loss of two thousand; the American loss was
trifling.

\* \* \*

HERE, in my rude log cabin,
Few poorer men there be
Among the mountain ranges
Of Eastern Tennessee.
My limbs are weak and shrunken,
White hairs upon my brow,
My dog lie still, old fellow!
My sole companion now.
Yet I, when young and lusty,
Have gone through stirring scenes,

For I went down with Carroll
To fight at New Orleans.

You say you'd like to hear me
The stirring story tell
Of those who stood the battle
And those who fighting fell.
Short work to count our losses
We stood and dropp'd the foe
As easily as by firelight
Men shoot the buck or doe.
And while they fell by hundreds
Upon the bloody plain,
Of us, fourteen were wounded,
And only eight were slain.

The eighth of January,
Before the break of day,
Our raw and hasty levies
Were brought into array.
No cotton-bales before us
Some fool that falsehood told;
Before us was an earthwork,
Built from the swampy mould.
And there we stood in silence,
And waited with a frown,
To greet with bloody welcome
The bulldogs of the Crown.

The heavy fog of morning
Still hid the plain from sight,
When came a thread of scarlet
Marked faintly in the white.
We fired a single cannon,
And as its thunders roll'd
The mist before us lifted

In many a heavy fold.
The mist before us lifted,
And in their bravery fine
Came rushing to their ruin
The fearless British line.

Then from our waiting cannons
Leap'd forth the deadly flame,
To meet the advancing columns
That swift and steady came.
The thirty-twos of Crowley
And Bluchi's twenty-four,
To Spotts's eighteen-pounders
Responded with their roar,
Sending the grape-shot deadly
That marked its pathway plain,
And paved the road it travell'd
With corpses of the slain.

Our rifles firmly grasping,
And heedless of the din,
We stood in silence waiting
For orders to begin.
Our fingers on the triggers,
Our hearts, with anger stirr'd,
Grew still more fierce and eager
As Jackson's voice was heard:
"Stand steady! Waste no powder
Wait till your shots will tell!
To-day the work you finish
See that you do it well!"

Their columns drawing nearer,
We felt our patience tire,
When came the voice of Carroll,
Distinct and measured, "Fire!"

Oh! then you should have mark'd us
Our volleys on them pour
Have heard our joyous rifles
Ring sharply through the roar,
And seen their foremost columns
Melt hastily away
As snow in mountain gorges
Before the floods of May.

They soon reformed their columns,
And 'mid the fatal rain
We never ceased to hurtle
Came to their work again.
The Forty-fourth is with them,
That first its laurels won
With stout old Abercrombie
Beneath an eastern sun.
It rushes to the battle,
And, though within the rear
Its leader is a laggard,
It shows no signs of fear.

It did not need its colonel,
For soon there came instead
An eagle-eyed commander,
And on its march he led.
'Twas Pakenham, in person,
The leader of the field;
I knew it by the cheering
That loudly round him peal'd;
And by his quick, sharp movement,
We felt his heart was stirr'd,
As when at Salamanca,
He led the fighting Third.

I raised my rifle quickly,

I sighted at his breast,
God save the gallant leader
And take him to his rest!
I did not draw the trigger,
I could not for my life.
So calm he sat his charger
Amid the deadly strife,
That in my fiercest moment
A prayer arose from me,-
God save that gallant leader,
Our foeman though he be.

Sir Edward's charger staggers:
He leaps at once to ground,
And ere the beast falls bleeding
Another horse is found.
His right arm falls - 'tis wounded;

He waves on high his left;
In vain he leads the movement,
The ranks in twain are cleft.
The men in scarlet waver
Before the men in brown,
And fly in utter panic
The soldiers of the Crown!

I thought the work was over,
But nearer shouts were heard,
And came, with Gibbs to head it,
The gallant Ninety-third.
Then Pakenham, exulting,
With proud and joyous glance,
Cried, "Children of the tartan-
Bold Highlanders advance!
Advance to scale the breastworks
And drive them from their hold,

And show the staunchless courage
That mark'd your sires of old!"

His voice as yet was ringing,
When, quick as light, there came
The roaring of a cannon,
And earth seemed all aflame.
Who causes thus the thunder
The doom of men to speak?
It is the Baritarian,
The fearless Dominique.
Down through the marshall'd Scotsmen
The step of death is heard,
And by the fierce tornado
Falls half the Ninety-third.

The smoke passed slowly upward,
And, as it soared on high,
I saw the brave commander
In dying anguish lie.
They bear him from the battle
Who never fled the foe;
Unmoved by death around them
His bearers softly go.
In vain their care, so gentle,
Fades earth and all its scenes;
The man of Salamanca
Lies dead at New Orleans.

But where were his lieutenants?
Had they in terror fled?
No! Keane was sorely wounded
And Gibbs as good as dead.
Brave Wilkinson commanding,
A major of brigade,
The shatter'd force to rally,

A final effort made.
He led it up our ramparts,
Small glory did he gain
Our captives some, while others fled,
And he himself was slain.

The stormers had retreated,
The bloody work was o'er;
The feet of the invaders
Were seen to leave our shore.
We rested on our rifles
And talk'd about the fight,
When came a sudden murmur
Like fire from left to right;
We turned and saw our chieftain,
And then, good friend of mine,
You should have heard the cheering
That rang along the line.

For well our men remembered
How little when they came,
Had they but native courage,
And trust in Jackson's name;
How through the day he labored,
How kept the vigils still,
Till discipline controlled us,
A stronger power than will;
And how he hurled us at them
Within the evening hour,
That red night in December,
And made us feel our power.

In answer to our shouting
Fire lit his eye of gray;
Erect, but thin and pallid,
He passed upon his bay.

Weak from the baffled fever,
And shrunken in each limb,
The swamps of Alabama
Had done their work on him.
But spite of that and lasting,
And hours of sleepless care,
The soul of Andrew Jackson
Shone forth in glory there.

# THE PICKET GUARD

## ETHEL LYNN BEERS

September, 1861

The stereotyped announcement, "All Quiet on the Potomac" was
followed one day in September, 1861, by the words, "A Picket
Shot," and these so moved the authoress that she wrote this
poem on the impulse of the moment.

\* \* \*

"ALL quiet along the Potomac," they say,
"Except now and then a stray picket
Is shot, as he walks on his beat, to and fro,
By a rifleman hid in the thicket.
'Tis nothing a private or two, now and then,
Will not count in the news of the battle;
Not an officer lost only one of the men,
Moaning out, all alone, the death rattle."

All quiet along the Potomac to-night,
Where the soldiers lie peacefully dreaming;
Their tents in the rays of the clear autumn moon,
Or the light of the watch-fires, are gleaming.

A tremulous sigh, as the gentle night-wind
Through the forest-leaves softly is creeping;
While stars up above, with their glittering eyes,
Keep guard for the army is sleeping.

There's only the sound of the lone sentry's tread,
As he tramps from the rock to the fountain,
And thinks of the two in the low trundle-bed
Far away in the cot on the mountain.
His musket falls slack his face, dark and grim,
Grows gentle with memories tender,
As he mutters a prayer for the children asleep
For their mother may Heaven defend her!

The moon seems to shine just as brightly as then,
That night, when the love yet unspoken
Leaped up to his lips when low-murmured vows
Were pledged to be ever unbroken.
Then drawing his sleeve roughly over his eyes,
He dashes off tears that are welling,
And gathers his gun closer up to its place
As if to keep down the heart-swelling.

He passes the fountain, the blasted pine-tree
The footstep is lagging and weary;
Yet onward he goes, through the broad belt of light,
Toward the shades of the forest so dreary.
Hark! was it the night-wind that rustled the leaves?
Was it moonlight so wondrously flashing?
It looked like a rifle "Ah! Mary, good-bye!"
And the life-blood is ebbing and plashing.

All quiet along the Potomac to-night,
No sound save the rush of the river;
While soft falls the dew on the face of the dead
The picket's off duty forever.

# THE LITTLE BLACK EYED REBEL

## WILL CARLETON

Between September 26th, 1777, and June 17th, 1778

The heroine's name was Mary Redmond, and she lived in Philadelphia. During the occupation of that town by the British, she was ever ready to aid in the secret delivery of the letters written home by the husbands and fathers fighting in the Continental Army.

\* \* \*

A BOY drove into the city, his wagon loaded down
With food to feed the people of the British-governed
    town;
And the little black-eyed rebel, so innocent and sly,
Was watching for his coming from the corner of her eye.

His face looked broad and honest, his hands were brown
    and tough,
The clothes he wore upon him were homespun, coarse,
    and rough;
But one there was who watched him, who long time
    lingered nigh,

And cast at him sweet glances from the corner of her eye.

He drove up to the market, he waited in the line;
His apples and potatoes were fresh and fair and fine;
But long and long he waited, and no one came to buy,
Save the black-eyed rebel, watching from the corner of
    her eye.

"Now who will buy my apples?" he shouted, long and
    loud;
And "Who wants my potatoes?" he repeated to the
    crowd;
But from all the people round him came no word of a
    reply,
Save the black-eyed rebel, answering from the corner of
    her eye.

For she knew that 'neath the lining of the coat he wore
    that day,
Were long letters from the husbands and the fathers far
    away,
Who were fighting for the freedom that they meant to
    gain or die;
And a tear like silver glistened in the corner of her eye.

But the treasures how to get them? crept the question
    through her mind,
Since keen enemies were watching for what prizes they
    might find:
And she paused a while and pondered, with a pretty little
    sigh;
Then resolve crept through her features, and a
    shrewdness fired her eye.

So she resolutely walked up to the wagon old and red;
"May I have a dozen apples for a kiss?" she sweetly said:

And the brown face flushed to scarlet; for the boy was
    somewhat shy,
And he saw her laughing at him from the corner of
    her eye.

"You may have them all for nothing, and more, if you
    want," quoth he.
"I will have them, my good fellow, but can pay for
    them,"said she;
And she clambered on the wagon, minding not who all
    were by,
With a laugh of reckless romping in the corner of her eye.

Clinging round his brawny neck, she clasped her fingers
    white and small,
And then whispered, "Quick! the letters! thrust them
    underneath my shawl!
Carry back again this package, and be sure that you are
    spry!"
And she sweetly smiled upon him from the corner of
    her eye.

Loud the motley crowd were laughing at the strange,
    ungirlish freak,
And the boy was scared and panting, and so dashed he
    could not speak;
And, "Miss, 7 have good apples," a bolder lad did cry;
But she answered, "No, I thank you," from the corner of
    her eye.

With the news of loved ones absent to the dear friends
    they would greet,
Searching them who hungered for them, swift she glided
    through the street.
"There is nothing worth the doing that it does not pay to
    try,"

Thought the little black-eyed rebel, with a twinkle in
   her eye.

# APOCALYPSE

## RICHARD REALF

April 19, 1861

The first life lost in the battle with rebellion was that of Private
Arthur Ladd, of the Sixth Massachusetts, killed in the attack of
the Baltimore mob.

\* \* \*

STRAIGHT to his heart the bullet crushed;
Down from his breast the red blood gushed,
And o'er his face a glory rushed.

A sudden spasm shook his frame,
And in his ears there went and came
A sound as of devouring flame.

Which in a moment ceased, and then
The great light clasped his brows again,
So that they shone like Stephen's when

Saul stood apart a little space
And shook with shuddering awe to trace

God's splendors settling o'er his face.

Thus, like a king, erect in pride,
Raising clean hands toward heaven, he cried;
"All hail the Stars and Stripes!" and died.

Died grandly. But before he fell
(O blessedness ineffable!)
Vision apocalyptical

Was granted to him, and his eyes,
All radiant with glad surprise,
Looked forward through the Centuries,

And saw the seeds which sages cast
In the world's soil in cycles past,
Spring up and blossom at the last;

Saw how the souls of men had grown,
And where the scythes of Truth had mown
Clear space for Liberty's white throne;

Saw how, by sorrow tried and proved,
The blackening stains had been removed
Forever from the land he loved;

Saw Treason crushed and Freedom crowned,
And clamorous Faction, gagged and bound,
Gasping its life out on the ground.

With far-off vision gazing clear
Beyond this gloomy atmosphere
Which shuts us out with doubt and fear

He marking how her high increase
Ran greatening in perpetual lease

Through balmy years of odorous Peace

Greeted in one transcendent cry
Of intense, passionate ecstasy
The sight which thrilled him utterly;

Saluting, with most proud disdain
Of murder and of mortal pain,
The vision which shall be again!

So, lifted with prophetic pride,
Raised conquering hands to heaven and cried:
"All hail the Stars and Stripes!" and died.

# SONG OF MARION'S MEN

## WILLIAM CULLEN BRYANT

1780 - 1781

While the British Army held South Carolina, Marion and
Sumter gathered bands of partisans and waged a vigorous
guerrilla warfare most harassing and destructive to the invader.

\* \* \*

OUR band is few, but true and tried,
Our leader frank and bold;
The British soldier trembles
When Marion's name is told.
Our fortress is the good greenwood
Our tent the cypress-tree;
We know the forest round us,
As seamen know the sea.
We know its walls of thorny vines,
Its glades of reedy grass,
Its safe and silent islands
Within the dark morass.

Woe to the English soldiery,

That little dread us near!
On them shall light at midnight
A strange and sudden fear:
When, waking to their tents on fire,
They grasp their arms in vain,
And they who stand to face us
Are beat to earth again.
And they who fly in terror deem
A mighty host behind,
And hear the tramp of thousands
Upon the hollow wind.

Then sweet the hour that brings release
From danger and from toil;
We talk the battle over,
And share the battle's spoil.
The woodland rings with laugh and shout
As if a hunt were up,
And woodland flowers are gathered
To crown the soldier's cup.
With merry songs we mock the wind
That in the pine-top grieves,
And slumber long and sweetly
On beds of oaken leaves.

Well knows the fair and friendly moon
The band that Marion leads
The glitter of their rifles,
The scampering of their steeds.
'Tis life to guide the fiery barb
Across the moonlight plain;
'Tis life to feel the night-wind
That lifts his tossing mane.
A moment in the British camp
A moment and away
Back to the pathless forest,

Before the peep of day.

Grave men there are by broad Santee,
Grave men with hoary hairs;
Their hearts are all with Marion,
For Marion are their prayers.
And lovely ladies greet our band
With kindliest welcoming,
With smiles like those of summer,
And tears like those of spring.
For them we wear these trusty arms,
And lay them down no more
Till we have driven the Briton,
Forever, from our shore.

# THE BAY-FIGHT

## HENRY HOWARD BROWNELL

August 5, 1864

The poet was acting ensign on the staff of Admiral Farragut, when he led his squadron past Forts Morgan and Gaines, and into a victorious fight with the Confederate fleet in the Bay of Mobile. The poem is here somewhat shortened.

\* \* \*

THREE days through sapphire seas we sailed,
The steady Trade blew strong and free,
The Northern Light his banners paled,
The Ocean Stream our channels wet,
We rounded low Canaveral's lee,
And passed the isles of emerald set
In blue Bahama's turquoise sea.

By reef and shoal obscurely mapped,
And hauntings of the gray sea-wolf,
The palmy Western Key lay lapped
In the warm washing of the Gulf.

But weary to the hearts of all
The burning glare, the barren reach
Of Santa Rosa's withered beach,
And Pensacola's ruined wall.

And weary was the long patrol,
The thousand miles of shapeless strand,
From Brazos to San Bias that roll
Their drifting dunes of desert sand.

Yet, coast-wise as we cruised or lay,
The land-breeze still at nightfall bore,
By beach and fortress-guarded bay,
Sweet odors from the enemy's shore,

Fresh from the forest solitudes,
Unchallenged of his sentry lines
The bursting of his cypress buds,
And the warm fragrance of his pines.

Ah, never braver bark and crew,
Nor bolder Flag a foe to dare.
Had left a wake on ocean blue
Since Lion-Heart sailed Trenc-le-mer!

But little gain by that dark ground
Was ours, save, sometime, freer breath
For friend or brother strangely found,
'Scaped from the drear domain of death.

And little venture for the bold,
Or laurel for our valiant Chief,
Save some blockaded British thief,
Full fraught with murder in his hold,

Caught unawares at ebb or flood—

Or dull bombardment, day by day,
With fort and earth-work, far away,
Low couched in sullen leagues of mud.

A weary time, but to the strong
The day at last, as ever, came;
And the volcano, laid so long,
Leaped forth in thunder and in flame!

Man your starboard battery!
Kimberly shouted
The ship, with her hearts of oak,
Was going, mid roar and smoke,
On to victory!
None of us doubted
No, not our dying
Farragut's flag was flying!

Gaines growled low on our left,
Morgan roared on our right
Before us, gloomy and fell,
With breath like the fume of hell,
Lay the Dragon of iron shell,
Driven at last to the fight!

Ha, old ship! do they thrill,
The brave two hundred scars
You got in the River- Wars?
That were leeched with clamorous skill,
(Surgery savage and hard),

Splinted with bolt and beam,
Probed in scarfing and seam,
Rudely linted and tarred
With oakum and boiling pitch,
And sutured with splice and hitch

At the Brooklyn Navy-Yard!

Our lofty spars were down,
To bide the battle's frown
(Wont of old renown) -
But every ship was drest
In her bravest and her best,
As if for a July day;
Sixty flags and three,
As we floated up the bay
Every peak and mast-head flew
The brave Red, White, and Blue-
We were eighteen ships that day.

With hawsers strong and taut,
The weaker lashed to port,
On we sailed, two by two
That if either a bolt should feel
Crash through caldron or wheel,
Fin of bronze or sinew of steel,
Her mate might bear her through.

Steadily nearing the head,
The great Flag-Ship led,
Grandest of sights!
On her lofty mizzen flew
Our Leader's dauntless Blue,
That had waved o'er twenty fights
So we went, with the first of the tide,
Slowly, mid the roar
Of the Rebel guns ashore
And the thunder of each full broadside.

Ah, how poor the prate
Of statute and state,
We once held with these fellows

Here, on the flood's pale-green,
Hark how he bellows,
Each bluff old Sea-Lawyer!
Talk to them, Dahlgren,
Parrott, and Sawyer!

On, in the whirling shade
Of the cannon's sulphury breath,
We drew to the Line of Death
That our devilish Foe had laid-
Meshed in a horrible net,
And baited villainous well,
Right in our path were set
Three hundred traps of hell!

And there, O sight forlorn!
There, while the cannon
Hurtled and thundered-
(Ah, what ill raven
Flapped o'er the ship that morn!)
Caught by the under-death,
In the drawing of a breath,
Down went dauntless Craven,
He and his hundred!

A moment we saw her turret,
A little heel she gave,
And a thin white spray went o'er her,
Like the crest of a breaking wave-
In that great iron coffin,
The channel for their grave,
The fort their monument,
(Seen afar in the offing,)
Ten fathom deep lie Craven,
And the bravest of our brave.

Then, in that deadly track,
A little the ships held back,
Closing up in their stations-
There are minutes that fix the fate
Of battles and of nations
(Christening the generations,)
When valor were all too late,
If a moment's doubt be harbored
From the main-top, bold and brief,
Came the word of our grand old Chief-
"Go on!" - 'twas all he said-
Our helm was put to the starboard,
And the Hartford passed ahead.

Ahead lay the Tennessee,
On our starboard bow he lay,
With his mail-clad consorts three,
(The rest had run up the Bay)-
There he was, belching flame from his bow,
And the steam from his throat's abyss
Was a Dragon's maddened hiss-
In sooth a most cursed craft!
In a sullen ring at bay
By the Middle Ground they lay,
Raking us fore and aft.

Trust me, our berth was hot,
Ah, wickedly well they shot;
How their death-bolts howled and stung!
And the water-batteries played
With their deadly cannonade
Till the air around us rung;
So the battle raged and roared
Ah, had you been aboard
To have seen the fight we made!
How they leaped, the tongues of flame,

From the cannon's fiery lip!
How the broadsides, deck and frame,
Shook the great ship!

And how the enemy's shell
Came crashing, heavy and oft,
Clouds of splinters flying aloft
And falling in oaken showers
But ah, the pluck of the crew!
Had you stood on that deck of ours
You had seen what men may do.

Still, as the fray grew louder,
Boldly they worked and well;
Steadily came the powder,
Steadily came the shell.
And if tackle or truck found hurt,
Quickly they cleared the wreck;
And the dead were laid to port,
All a-row, on our deck.

Never a nerve that failed,
Never a cheek that paled,
Not a tinge of gloom or pallor-
There was bold Kentucky's grit,
And the old Virginian valor,
And the daring Yankee wit.

There were blue eyes from turfy Shannon,
There were black orbs from palmy soldier-
But there, alongside the cannon,
Each man fought like a tiger!

A little, once, it looked ill,
Our consort began to burn
They quenched the flames with a will,

But our men were falling still,
And still the fleet was astern.

Right abreast of the Fort
In an awful shroud they lay,
Broadsides thundering away,
And lightning from every port-
Scene of glory and dread!

A storm-cloud all aglow
With flashes of fiery red
The thunder raging below,
And the forest of flags o'erhead!

So grand the hurly and roar,
So fiercely their broadsides blazed,
The regiments fighting ashore
Forgot to fire as they gazed.

There, to silence the Foe,
Moving grimly and slow,
They loomed in that deadly wreath,
Where the darkest batteries frowned
Death in the air all round,
And the black torpedoes beneath!

And now, as we looked ahead,
All for'ard, the long white deck
Was growing a strange dull red;
But soon, as once and agen
Fore and aft we sped
(The firing to guide or check,)
You could hardly choose but tread
On the ghastly human wreck,
(Dreadful gobbet and shred
That a minute ago were men!)

Red, from mainmast to bitts!
Red, on bulwark and wale-
Red, by combing and hatch
Red, o'er netting and rail!

And ever, with steady con,
The ship forged slowly by
And ever the crew fought on,
And their cheers rang loud and high.

Grand was the sight to see
How by their guns they stood,
Right in front of our dead
Fighting square abreast-
Each brawny arm and chest
All spotted with black and red,
Chrism of fire and blood!

Worth our watch, dull and sterile,
Worth all the weary time-
Worth the woe and the peril,
To stand in that strait sublime!

Fear? A forgotten form!
Death? A dream of the eyes!
We were atoms in God's great storm
That roared through the angry skies.

One only doubt was ours,
One only dread we knew-
Could the day that dawned so well
Go down for the Darker Powers?
Would the fleet get through?
And ever the shot and shell
Came with the howl of hell,
The splinter-clouds rose and fell,

And the long line of corpses grew
Would the fleet win through?

They are men that never will fail
(How aforetime they've fought!)
But Murder may yet prevail-
They may sink as Craven sank.
Therewith one hard, fierce thought,
Burning on heart and lip,
Ran like fire through the ship
Fight her, to the last plank!

A dimmer Renown might strike
If Death lay square alongside
But the Old Flag has no like,
She must fight, whatever betide
When the war is a tale of old,
And this day's story is told,
They shall hear how the Hartford died!

But as we ranged ahead,
And the leading ships worked in,
Losing their hope to win,
The enemy turned and fled
And one seeks a shallow reach,
And another, winged in her flight,
Our mate, brave Jouett, brings in
And one, all torn in the fight,
Runs for a wreck on the beach,
Where her flames soon fire the night.

And the Ram, when well up the Bay,
And we looked that our stems should meet,
(He had us fair for a prey,)
Shifting his helm midway,
Sheered off and ran for the fleet;

There, without skulking or sham,
He fought them, gun for gun,
And ever he sought to ram,
But could finish never a one.

From the first of the iron shower
Till we sent our parting shell,
'Twas just one savage hour
Of the roar and the rage of hell.

With the lessening smoke and thunder,
Our glasses around we aim
What is that burning yonder?
Our Philippi, aground and in flame!

Below, 'twas still all a-roar,
As the ships went by the shore,
But the fire of the fort had slacked,
(So fierce their volleys had been)
And now, with a mighty din,
The whole fleet came grandly in,
Though sorely battered and wracked.

So, up the Bay we ran,
The Flag to port and ahead,
And a pitying rain began
To wash the lips of our dead.

A league from the Fort we lay,
And deemed that the end must lag;
When lo! looking down the Bay,
There flaunted the Rebel Rag
The Ram is again under way,
And heading dead for the Flag!

Steering up with the stream,

94

Boldly his course he lay,
Though the fleet all answered his fire,
And, as he still drew nigher,
Ever on bow and beam
Our Monitors pounded away-
How the Chickasaw hammered away!

Quickly breasting the wave,
Eager the prize to win,
First of us all the brave
Monongahela went in
Under full head of steam-
Twice she struck him abeam,
Till her stem was a sorry work,
(She might have run on a crag!)
The Lackawanna hit fair,
He flung her aside like cork,
And still he held for the Flag.

High in the mizzen shroud
(Lest the smoke his sight o'erwhelm),
Our Admiral's voice rang loud,:
"Hard-a-starboard your helm!
Starboard! and run him down!"
Starboard it was and so,
Like a black squall's lifting frown,
Our mighty bow bore down
On the iron beak of the Foe.

We stood on the deck together,
Men that had looked on death
In battle and stormy weather-
Yet a little we held our breath,
When, with the hush of death,
The great ships drew together.

Our Captain strode to the bow,
Drayton, courtly and wise,
Kindly cynic, and wise,
(You hardly had known him now,
The flame of fight in his eyes!)
His brave heart eager to feel
How the oak would tell on the steel!

But, as the space grew short,
A little he seemed to shun us,
Out peered a form grim and lanky,
And a voice yelled: "Hard-a-port!
Hard-a-port! here's the damned Yankee
Coming right down on us!"

He sheered, but the ships ran foul;
With a gnarring shudder and growl
He gave us a deadly gun;
But as he passed in his pride,
(Rasping right alongside!)
The Old Flag, in thunder tones,
Poured in her port broadside,
Rattling his iron hide,
And cracking his timber bones!

Just then, at speed on the Foe,
With her bow all weathered and brown,
The great Lackawanna came down,
Full tilt, for another blow;
We were forging ahead,
She reversed but, for all our pains,
Rammed the old Hartford instead,
Just for'ard the mizzen-chains!

Ah! how the masts did buckle and bend,
And the stout hull ring and reel,

As she took us right on end!
(Vain were engine and wheel,
She was under full steam)-
With the roar of a thunder-stroke
Her two thousand tons of oak
Brought up on us, right abeam!

A wreck, as it looked, we lay
(Rib and plankshear gave way
To the stroke of that giant wedge!)
Here, after all, we go
The old ship is gone! ah, no,
But cut to the water's edge.

Never mind then at him again!
His flurry now can't last long;
He'll never again see land-
Try that on him, Marchand!
On him again, brave Strong!

Heading square at the hulk,
Full on his beam we bore;
But the spine of the huge Sea-Hog
Lay on the tide like a log,
He vomited flame no more.

By this he had found it hot-
Half the fleet, in an angry ring,
Closed round the hideous Thing,
Hammering with solid shot,

And bearing down, bow on bow-
He had but a minute to choose;
Life or renown? which now
Will the Rebel Admiral lose?

Cruel, haughty, and cold,
He ever was strong and bold-
Shall he shrink from a wooden stem?
He will think of that brave band
He sank in the Cumberland-
Ay, he will sink like them.

Nothing left but to fight
Boldly his last sea-fight!
Can he strike? By heaven, 'tis true!
Down comes the traitor Blue,
And up goes the captive White!

Up went the White! Ah then
The hurrahs that, once and agen,
Rang from three thousand men
All flushed and savage with fight!

Our dead lay cold and stark,
But our dying, down in the dark,
Answered as best they might
Lifting their poor lost arms,
And cheering for God and Right!

# CRAVEN

## HENRY NEWBOLT

August 5, 1864

In the attack on Mobile Bay the monitor Tecumseh was sunk by
a torpedo.

\* \* \*

OVER the turret, shut in his iron-clad tower,
Craven was conning his ship through smoke and
flame;
Gun to gun he had battered the fort for an hour,
Now was the time for a charge to end the game.

There lay the narrowing channel, smooth and grim,
A hundred deaths beneath it, and never a sign;
There lay the enemy's ships, and sink or swim
The flag was flying, and he was head of the line.

The fleet behind was jamming; the monitor hung
Beating the stream; the roar for a moment hushed,
Craven spoke to the pilot; slow she swung;
Again he spoke, and right for the foe she rushed.

Into the narrowing channel, between the shore
And the sunk torpedoes lying in treacherous rank;
She turned but a yard too short; a muffled roar,
A mountainous wave, and she rolled, righted, and sank.

Over the manhole, up in the iron-clad tower,
Pilot and Captain met as they turned to fly:
The hundredth part of a moment seemed an hour,
For one could pass to be saved, and one must die.

They stood like men in a dream: Craven spoke,
Spoke as he lived and fought, with a Captain's pride,
"After you, Pilot." The pilot woke,
Down the ladder he went, and Craven died.

All men praise the deed and the manner, but we-
We set it apart from the pride that stoops to the proud,
The strength that is supple to serve the strong and free,
The grace of the empty hands and promises loud:

Sidney thirsting, a humbler need to slake,
Nelson waiting his turn for the surgeon's hand,
Lucas crushed with chains for a comrade's sake,
Outram coveting right before command:

These were paladins, these were Craven's peers,
These with him shall be crowned in story and song,
Crowned with the glitter of steel and the glimmer of tears,
Princes of courtesy, merciful, proud, and strong.

# OLD IRONSIDES

## OLIVER WENDELL HOLMES

September 16th, 1830

The frigate Constitution was launched in 1797, and took part in the war with Tripoli in 1804. In 1812 she captured the British Guerriere on August 19th, and the British Java on December 29th. After the war she served as a training ship. In 1830 it was proposed to break her up, which called forth this indignant poem. In 1876 she was refitted, and in 1878 she took over the American exhibits to the Paris Exhibition. She now lies out of commission in Rotten Row, at the Brooklyn Navy Yard.

A, tear her tattered ensign down!
Long has it waved on high,
And many an eye has danced to see
That banner in the sky;
Beneath it rung the battle shout,
And burst the cannon's roar;
The meteor of the ocean air
Shall sweep the clouds no more!

Her deck, once red with heroes' blood,
　　Where knelt the vanquished foe,
When winds were hurrying o'er the flood
　　And waves were white below,
　No more shall feel the victor's tread,
　　Or know the conquered knee;
　The harpies of the shore shall pluck
　　The eagle of the sea!

　Oh, better that her shattered hulk
　　Should sink beneath the wave;
Her thunders shook the mighty deep,
　　And there should be her grave;
　Nail to the mast her holy flag,
　　Set every threadbare sail,
　And give her to the God of storms,
　　The lightning and the gale!

# MOLLY MAGUIRE AT MONMOUTH

## WILLIAM COLLINS

June 28th, 1778

The battle of Monmouth was indecisive, but the Americans held the field, and the British retreated and remained inactive for the rest of the summer.

ON the bloody field of Monmouth
Flashed the guns of Greene and Wayne.
Fiercely roared the tide of battle,
Thick the sward was heaped with slain.
Foremost, facing death and danger,
Hessian, horse, and grenadier,
In the vanguard, fiercely fighting,
Stood an Irish Cannoneer.

Loudly roared his iron cannon,
Mingling ever in the strife,
And beside him, firm and daring,
Stood his faithful Irish wife.

Of her bold contempt of danger
Greene and Lee's Brigades could tell,
Every one knew "Captain Molly,"
And the army loved her well.

Surged the roar of battle round them,
Swiftly flew the iron hail,
Forward dashed a thousand bayonets,
That lone battery to assail.
From the foeman's foremost columns
Swept a furious fusillade,
Mowing down the massed battalions
In the ranks of Greene's Brigade.

Fast and faster worked the gunner,
Soiled with powder, blood, and dust,
English bayonets shone before him,
Shot and shell around him burst;
Still he fought with reckless daring,
Stood and manned her long and well,
Till at last the gallant fellow
Dead beside his cannon fell.

With a bitter cry of sorrow,
And a dark and angry frown,
Looked that band of gallant patriots
At their gunner stricken down.
"Fall back, comrades, it is folly
Thus to strive against the foe."
"No! not so," cried Irish Molly;
'We can strike another blow."

Quickly leaped she to the cannon,
In her fallen husband's place,
Sponged and rammed it fast and steady,

Fired it in the foeman's face.
Flashed another ringing volley,
Roared another from the gun;
"Boys, hurrah!" cried gallant Molly,
"For the flag of Washington."

Greene's Brigade, though shorn and shattered,
Slain and bleeding half their men,
When they heard that Irish slogan,
Turned and charged the foe again.
Knox and Wayne and Morgan rally,
To the front they forward wheel,
And before their rushing onset
Clinton's English columns reel.

Still the cannon's voice in anger
Rolled and rattled o'er the plain,
Till there lay in swarms around it
Mangled heaps of Hessian slain.
"Forward! charge them with the bayonet!"
'Twas the voice of Washington,
And there burst a fiery greeting
From the Irish woman's gun.

Monckton falls; against his columns
Leap the troops of Wayne and Lee,
And before their reeking bayonets
Clinton's red battalions flee.
Morgan's rifles, fiercely flashing,
Thin the foe's retreating ranks,
And behind them onward dashing
Ogden hovers on their flanks.

Fast they fly, these boasting Britons,
Who in all their glory came,

With their brutal Hessian hirelings
To wipe out our country's name.
Proudly floats the starry banner,
Monmouth's glorious field is won,
And in triumph Irish Molly
Stands beside her smoking gun.

# GRANT

## H. C. BUNNER

1822, 1885

This was written on the day of Grant's death,
July 23rd.

\* \* \*

SMILE on, thou new-come Spring if on thy breeze
The breath of a great man go wavering up
And out of this world's knowledge, it is well.

Kindle with thy green flame the stricken trees,
And fire the rose's many-petaled cup,
Let bough and branch with quickening life-blood swell
But Death shall touch his spirit with a life
That knows not years or seasons. Oh, how small
Thy little hour of bloom! Thy leaves shall fall,
And be the sport of winter winds at strife;
But he has taken on eternity.
Yea, of how much this Death doth set him free!
Now are we one to love him, once again.

The tie that bound him to our bitterest pain
Draws him more close to Love and Memory.

O Spring, with all thy sweetheart frolics, say,
Hast thou remembrance of those earlier springs
When we wept answer to the laughing day,
And turned aside from green and gracious things?
There was a sound of weeping over all-
Mothers uncomforted, for their sons were not;
And there was crueler silence: tears grew hot
In the true eyes that would not let them fall.

Up from the South came a great wave of sorrow
That drowned our hearthstones, splashed with blood our sills;
To-day, that spared, made terrible To-morrow
With thick presentiment of coming ills.
Only we knew the Right but oh, how strong,
How pitiless, how insatiable the Wrong!

And then the quivering sword-hilt found a hand
That knew not how to falter or grow weak;
And we looked on, from end to end the land,
And felt the heart spring up, and rise afresh
The blood of courage to the whitened cheek,
And fire of battle thrill the numbing flesh.
Ay, there was death, and pain, and dear ones missed,
And lips forever to grow pale unkissed;
But lo, the man was here, and this was he;
And at his hands Faith gave us victory.

Spring, thy poor life, that mocks his body's death,
Is but a candle's flame, a flower's breath.
He lives in days that suffering made dear
Beyond all garnered beauty of the year.
He lives in all of us that shall outlive

The sensuous things that paltry time can give.
This Spring the spirit of his broken age
Across the threshold of its anguish stole
All of him that was noble, fearless, sage,
Lives in his loved nation's strengthened soul.

# 29

# HOW ARE YOU, SANITARY

## BRET HARTE

1861 - 1865

Early in the war, the U. S. Sanitary Commission was organized, to supply comforts to the soldier in the field from the voluntary contributions of the men and women at home. Out of this grew the Red-Cross Associations of Europe.

DOWN the picket-guarded lane
Rolled the comfort-laden wain,
Cheered by shouts that shook the plain,
Soldier-like and merry:
Phrases such as camps may teach,
Sabre-cuts of Saxon speech,
Such as "Bully!" "Them's the peach!"
"Wade in, Sanitary!"

Right and left the caissons drew
As the car went lumbering through,
Quick succeeding in review
Squadrons military;

Sunburnt men with beards like frieze,
Smooth-faced boys, and cries like these,
"U. S. San. Com." "That's the cheese!"
        "Pass in, Sanitary!"

In such cheer it struggled on
Till the battle front was won,
Then the car, its journey done,
        Lo! was stationary;
And where bullets whistling fly,
Came the sadder, fainter cry,
"Help us, brothers, ere we die,
        Save us, Sanitary!"

Such the work. The phantom flies,
Wrapped in battle clouds that rise;
But the brave whose dying eyes,
        Veiled and visionary,
See the jasper gates swung wide,
See the parted throng outside
Hears the voice to those who ride:
        "Pass in, Sanitary!"

# 30

# TO THE MEMORY OF THE AMERICANS WHO FELL AT EUTAW

### PHILIP FRENEAU

September 8th, 1781

The fight of Eutaw Springs, although called a drawn battle, resulted in the withdrawal of the British troops from South Carolina.

\* \* \*

A Eutaw Springs the valiant died:
Their limbs with dust are covered o'er
Weep on, ye springs, your tearful tide;
How many heroes are no more!

If, in this wreck of ruin, they
Can yet be thought to claim the tear,
Oh, smite your gentle breast, and say,
The friends of freedom slumber here!

Thou, who shalt trace this bloody plain,
If goodness rules thy generous breast,
Sigh for the wasted rural reign;
Sigh for the shepherds, sunk to rest!

Stranger, their humble graves adorn;
You too may fall, and ask a tear;
'Tis not the beauty of the morn
That proves the evening shall be clear,

They saw their injure'd country's woe;
The flaming town, the wasted field;
Then rush'd to meet the insulting foe;
They took the spear but left the shield.

Led by thy conquering genius, Greene,
The Britons they compelled to fly:
None distant view'd the fatal plain,
None griev'd, in such a cause, to die,

But, like the Parthians, fam'd of old,
Who, flying, still their arrows threw;
These routed Britons, full as bold
Retreated, and retreating slew.

Now rest in peace, our patriot band;
Though far from Nature's limits thrown,
We trust they find a happier land,
A brighter sunshine of their own.

# GEORGE WASHINGTON

## JAMES RUSSELL LOWELL

July 8th, 1775

This is a fragment from the ode for the centenary of
Washington's taking command of the American army at
Cambridge.

SOLDIER and statesman, rarest unison;
High-poised example of great duties done
Simply as breathing, a world's honors worn
As life's indifferent gifts to all men born;
Dumb for himself, unless it were to God,
But for his barefoot soldiers eloquent,
Tramping the snow to coral where they trod,
Held by his awe in hollow-eyed content;
Modest, yet firm as Nature's self; unblamed
Save by the men his nobler temper shamed;
Never seduced through show of present good
By other than unsetting lights to steer
New-trimmed in Heaven, nor than his steadfast mood
More steadfast, far from rashness as from fear,

Rigid, but with himself first, grasping still
In swerveless poise the wave-beat helm of will;
Not honored then or now because he wooed
The popular voice, but that he still withstood;
Broad-minded, higher-souled, there is but one
Who was all this and ours, and all men's WASHINGTON.

# 32

# THE STAR-SPANGLED BANNER

## FRANCIS SCOTT KEY

September 14th, 1813

After the British had burned the Capitol at Washington, in
August, 1813, they retired to their ships, and on September 12th
and 13th, they made an attack on Baltimore. This poem was
written on the morning after the bombardment of Fort
McHenry, while the author was a prisoner on the British fleet.

\* \* \*

OH! say can you see, by the dawn's early light,
What so proudly we hailed at the twilight's last gleaming;

Whose broad stripes and bright stars through the perilous fight,
O'er the ramparts we watched, were so gallantly streaming?
And the rocket's red glare, the bombs bursting in air,
Gave proof through the night that our flag was still there;
Oh, say, does that star-spangled banner yet wave
O'er the land of the free and the home of the brave?

On the shore, dimly seen through the mists of the deep,
Where the foe's haughty host in dread silence reposes,

What is that which the breeze o'er the towering steep
As it fitfully blows, half conceals, hah discloses?
Now it catches the gleam of the morning's first beam;
Its full glory reflected now shines on the stream;
'Tis the star-spangled banner! Oh! long may it wave
O'er the land of the free and the home of the brave!

And where is the band who so vauntingly swore,
'Mid the havoc of war and the battle's confusion,
A home and a country they'd leave us no more?
Their blood hath washed out their foul footsteps' pollution;
No refuge could save the hireling and slave
From the terror of flight, or the gloom of the grave,
And the star-spangled banner in triumph doth wave
O'er the land of the free and the home of the brave!

Oh! thus be it ever, when freemen shall stand
Between their loved home and the war's desolation;
Blessed with victory and peace, may the Heaven-rescued land
Praise the Power that hath made and preserved us a nation.
Then conquer we must, for our cause it is just,
And this be our motto, "In God is our trust":
And the star-spangled banner in triumph shall wave
O'er the land of the free and the home of the brave!

# 33

# THE CUMBERLAND

## HENRY WADSWORTH LONGFELLOW

March 8, 1862

The "Cumberland" was sunk by the iron-clad rebel ram "Merrimac," going down with her colors flying, and firing even as the water rose over the gunwale.

* * *

AT anchor in Hampton Roads we lay,
On board of the Cumberland, sloop-of-war;
And at times from the fortress across the bay
The alarum of drums swept past,
Or a bugle blast
From the camp on the shore.

Then far away to the south uprose
A little feather of snow-white smoke,
And we knew that the iron ship of our foes
Was steadily steering its course
To try the force
Of our ribs of oak.

Down upon us heavily runs,
Silent and sullen, the floating fort;
Then comes a puff of smoke from her guns,
And leaps the terrible death,
With fiery breath,
From each open port.

We are not idle, but send her straight
Defiance back in a full broadside!
As hail rebounds from a roof of slate,
Rebounds our heavier hail
From each iron scale
Of the monster's hide.

"Strike your flag!" the rebel cries,
In his arrogant old plantation strain.
"Never!" our gallant Morris replies;
"It is better to sink than to yield!"
And the whole air pealed
With the cheers of our men.

Then, like a kraken huge and black,

She crushed our ribs in her iron grasp!
Down went the Cumberland all a wrack,
With a sudden shudder of death,
And the cannon's breath
For her dying gasp.

Next morn, as the sun rose over the bay,
Still floated our flag at the mainmast head.
Lord, how beautiful was Thy day!
Every waft of the air
Was a whisper of prayer,
Or a dirge for the dead.

Ho! brave hearts that went down in the seas!
Ye are at peace in the troubled stream;
Ho! brave land! with hearts like these,
Thy flag, that is rent in twain,
Shall be one again,
And without a seam!

# AT THE FARRAGUT STATUE

## ROBERT BRIDGES

1801, 1870

Farragufs statue by Saint Gaudens was unveiled in New York in
1881.

\* \* \*

TO live a hero, then to stand
In bronze serene above the city's throng;
Hero at sea, and now on land
Revered by thousands as they rush along;

If these were all the gifts of fame
To be a shade amid alert reality,
And win a statue and a name-
How cold and cheerless immortality!

But when the sun shines in the Square,
And multitudes are swarming in the street,
Children are always gathered there,
Laughing and playing round the hero's feet.

# PERRY'S VICTORY ON LAKE ERIE

## JAMES GATES PERCIVAL

September 10th, 1813

Throughout the war of 1812 with Great Britain, the navy was
more successful than the army. In the battle on Lake Erie,
Commodore Oliver Hazard Perry captured six British vessels.

\* \* \*

BRIGHT was the morn, the waveless bay
Shone like a mirror to the sun;
'Mid greenwood shades and meadows gay,
The matin birds their lays begun:
While swelling o'er the gloomy wood
Was heard the faintly-echoed roar,
The dashing of the foaming flood,
That beat on Erie's distant shore.

The tawny wanderer of the wild
Paddled his painted birch canoe,
And, where the wave serenely smiled,
Swift as the darting falcon, flew;
He rowed along that peaceful bay,

And glanced its polished surface o'er,
Listening the billow far away,
That rolled on Erie's lonely shore.

What sounds awake my slumbering ear,
What echoes o'er the waters come?
It is the morning gun I hear,
The rolling of the distant drum.
Far o'er the bright illumined wave
I mark the flash, I hear the roar,
That calls from sleep the slumbering brave,
To fight on Erie's lonely shore.

See how the starry banner floats,
And sparkles in the morning ray:
While sweetly swell the fife's gay notes
In echoes o'er the gleaming bay:
Flash follows flash, as through yon fleet
Columbia's cannons loudly roar,
And valiant tars the battle greet,
That storms on Erie's echoing shore.

O, who can tell what deeds were done,
When Britain's cross, on yonder wave,
Sunk 'neath Columbia's dazzling sun,
And met in Erie's flood its grave?
Who tell the triumphs of that day,
When, smiling at the cannon's roar,
Our hero, 'mid the bloody fray,
Conquered on Erie's echoing shore.

Though many a wounded bosom bleeds
For sire, for son, for lover dear,
Yet Sorrow smiles amid her weeds,
Affliction dries her tender tear;
Oh! she exclaims, with glowing pride,

With ardent thoughts that wildly soar,
My sire, my son, my lover died,
Conquering on Erie's bloody shore.

Long shall my country bless that day,
When soared our Eagle to the skies;
Long, long in triumph's bright array,
That victory shall proudly rise:
And when our country's lights are gone,
And all its proudest days are o'er,
How will her fading courage dawn,
To think on Erie's bloody shore!

# TO PEACE, WITH VICTORY

## CORINNE ROOSEVELT ROBINSON

November 11, 1918

* * *

I COULD not welcome you, oh! longed-for peace,
Unless your coming had been heralded
By victory. The legions who have bled
Had elsewise died in vain for our release.

But now that you come sternly, let me kneel
And pay my tribute to the myriad dead,
Who counted not the blood that they have shed
Against the goal their valor shall reveal.

Ah ! what had been the shame, had all the stars
And stripes of our brave flag drooped still unfurled,
When the fair freedom of the weary world
Hung in the balance. Welcome then the scars!

Welcome the sacrifice! With lifted head
Our nation greets dear Peace as honor's right;

And ye the Brave, the Fallen in the fight,
Had ye not perished, then were honor dead!

# HOW OLD BROWN TOOK HARPER'S FERRY

## EDMUND CLARENCE STEDMAN

October 16th - December 2nd, 1859

It was on Sunday, October 16th, that John Brown took the Arsenal at Harper's Ferry. On the 18th he was captured. On December 2nd he was hanged. One year later began the War which caused the abolition of slavery.

\* \* \*

JOHN BROWN in Kansas settled, like a steadfast Yankee farmer,
Brave and godly, with four sons, all stalwart men of might.
There he spoke aloud for freedom, and the Borderstrife grew warmer,
Till the Rangers fired his dwelling, in his absence, in the night;
And Old Brown
Osawatomie Brown,
Came homeward in the morning to find his house burned down.

Then he grasped his trusty rifle and boldly fought for
    freedom;
Smote from border unto border the fierce, invading band;
And he and his brave boys vowed so might Heaven help
    and speed 'em!
They would save those grand old prairies from the
    curse that
blights the land;
And Old Brown,
Osawatomie Brown,
Said, "Boys, the Lord will aid us!" and he shoved his ram
    rod down.

And the Lord did aid these men, and they labored day and
    even,
Saving Kansas from its peril; and their very lives seemed
    charmed,
Till the ruffians killed one son, in the blessed light of
    Heaven,
In cold blood the fellows slew him, as he journeyed all
    unarmed;
Then Old Brown,
Osawatomie Brown,
Shed not a tear, but shut his teeth, and frowned a terrible
    frown!

Then they seized another brave boy, not amid the heat of
    battle,
But in peace, behind his ploughshare, and they loaded
    him with chains,
And with pikes, before their horses, even as they goad
    their cattle,
Drove him cruelly, for their sport, and at last blew out his
    brains;
Then Old Brown,
Osawatomie Brown,

Raised his right hand up to Heaven, calling Heaven's
    vengeance down.

And he swore a fearful oath, by the name of the Almighty,
He would hunt this ravening evil that had scathed and
    torn him so;
He would seize it by the vitals; he would crush it day and
    night; he
Would so pursue its footsteps, so return it blow for blow,
That Old Brown,
Osawatomie Brown,
Should be a name to swear by, in backwoods or in town!

Then his beard became more grizzled, and his wild blue
    eye grew wilder,
And more sharply curved his hawk's-nose, snuffing battle
    from afar;
And he and the two boys left, though the Kansas strife
    waxed milder,
Grew more sullen, till was over the bloody Border War,
And Old Brown,
Osawatomie Brown,
Had gone crazy, as they reckoned by his fearful glare and
    frown.

So he left the plains of Kansas and their bitter woes
    behind him,
Slipt off into Virginia, where the statesmen all are born,
Hired a farm by Harper's Ferry, and no one knew where
    to find him,
Or whether he'd turned parson, or was jacketed and
    shorn;
For Old Brown,
Osawatomie Brown,
Mad as he was, knew texts enough to wear a parson's
    gown.

He bought no ploughs and harrows, spades and shovels,
and such trifles;
But quietly to his rancho there came, by every train,
Boxes full of pikes and pistols, and his well-beloved
Sharp's rifles;
And eighteen other madmen joined their leader there
again.
Says Old Brown,
Osawatomie Brown,
Boys, we've got an army large enough to march and take
the town!

Take the town, and seize the muskets, free the negroes
and then arm them;
Carry the County and the State, ay, and all the potent
South.
On their own heads be the slaughter, if their victims rise
to harm them
These Virginians! who believed not, nor would heed the
warning mouth.
Says Old Brown,
Osawatomie Brown,
The world shall see a Republic, or my name is not John
Brown.

Twas the sixteenth of October, on the evening of a
Sunday:
"This good work," declared the captain, shall be on a holy
night!
It was on a Sunday evening, and before the noon of
Monday,
With two sons, and Captain Stephens, fifteen privates
black and white,
Captain Brown,
Osawatoniie Brown,

Marched across the bridged Potomac, and knocked the
sentry down;

Took the guarded armory-building, and the muskets and
the cannon;
Captured all the county majors and the colonels, one
by one;
Scared to death each gallant scion of Virginia they ran on,
And before the noon of Monday, I say, the deed was done.
Mad Old Brown,
Osawatoniie Brown,
With his eighteen other crazy men, went in and took the
town.

Very little noise and bluster, little smell of powder
made he;
It was all done in the midnight, like the Emperor's coup
d'etat.
"Cut the wires! Stop the rail-cars! Hold the streets and
bridges!" said he,
Then declared the new Republic, with himself for guiding
star,
This Old Brown,
Osawatoniie Brown;
And the bold two thousand citizens ran off and left the
town.

Then was riding and railroading and expressing here and
thither;
And the Martinsburg Sharpshooters and the Charlestown
Volunteers,
And the Shepherdstown and Winchester Militia hastened
whither
Old Brown was said to muster his ten thousand grenadiers.
General Brown!

Osawatomie Brown!
Behind whose rampant banner all the North was pouring
    down.

But at last, 'tis said, some prisoners escaped from Old
    Brown's durance,
And the effervescent valor of the Chivalry broke out,
When they learned that nineteen madmen had the
    marvelous assurance-
Only nineteen thus to seize the place and drive them
    straight about;
And Old Brown,
Osawatomie Brown,
Found an army come to take him, encamped around the
    town.

But to storm, with all the forces I have mentioned, was
    too risky;
So they hurried off to Richmond for the Government
    Marines,
Tore them from their weeping matrons, fired their souls
    with Bourbon whiskey,
Till they battered down Brown's castle with their ladders
and machines;
And Old Brown,
Osawatomie Brown,
Received three bayonet stabs, and a cut on his brave old
    crown.

Tallyho! the old Virginia gentry gather to the baying!
In they rushed and killed the game, shooting lustily away;
And whene'er they slew a rebel, those who came too late
    for slaying,
Not to lose a share of glory, fired their bullets in his clay;
And Old Brown,
Osawatomie Brown,

Saw his sons fall dead beside him, and between them laid
    him down.

How the conquerors wore their laurels; how they
    hastened on the trial;
How Old Brown was placed, half dying, on the
    Charlestown court-house floor;
How he spoke his grand oration, in the scorn of all denial;
What the brave old madman told them, these are known
the country o'er.
"Hang Old Brown,
Osawatomie Brown."
Said the judge, "and all such rebels!" with his most judicial
    frown.

But, Virginians, don't do it! for I tell you that the flagon,
Filled with blood of Old Brown's offspring, was first
    poured by Southern hands;
And each drop from Old Brown's life-veins, like the red
    gore of the dragon,
May spring up a vengeful Fury, hissing through your
    slave-worn lands!
And Old Brown,
Osawatomie Brown,
May trouble you more than ever, when you've nailed his
    coffin down!

# O CAPTAIN! MY CAPTAIN!

## WALT WHITMAN

April 15th, 1865

Abraham Lincoln was killed by John Wilkes Booth, almost exactly four years after the first shot was fired at Fort Sumter.

\* \* \*

O CAPTAIN! my Captain! our fearful trip is done,
The ship has weather'd every rack, the prize we sought
is won;
The port is near, the bells I hear, the people all exulting,
While follow eyes the steady keel, the vessel grim and
daring:
But O heart! heart! heart!
O the bleeding drops of red,
Where on the deck my Captain lies,
Fallen cold and dead!

O Captain! my Captain! rise up and hear the bells;
Rise up for you the flag is flung for you the bugle trills;
For you bouquets and ribbon'd wreaths for you the
shores

a-crowding;
For you they call, the swaying mass, their eager faces
    turning;
Here, Captain! dear father!
This arm beneath your head;
It is some dream that on the deck
You've fallen cold and dead.

My Captain does not answer, his lips are pale and still;
My father does not feel my arm, he has no pulse nor will:
The ship is anchor'd safe and sound, its voyage closed and
    done;
From fearful trip the victor ship comes in with
    object won:
Exult, O shores, and ring, O bells!
But I, with mournful tread,
Walk the deck my Captain lies,
Fallen cold and dead.

# SONG OF THE SOLDIERS

## CHARLES G. HALPINE

1861 - 1865

\* \* \*

COMRADES known in marches many,
Comrades, tried in dangers many,
Comrades, bound by memories many,
Brothers let us be.
Wounds or sickness may divide us,
Marching orders may divide us,
But whatever fate betide us,
Brothers of the heart are we.

Comrades, known by faith the clearest,
Tried when death was near and nearest,
Bound we are by ties the dearest,
Brothers evermore to be.
And, if spared, and growing older,
Shoulder still in line with shoulder,
And with hearts no thrill the colder,
Brothers ever we shall be.

By communion of the banner,
Crimson, white, and starry banner,
By the baptism of the banner,
Children of one Church are we.
Creed nor faction can divide us,
Race nor language can divide us
Still, whatever fate betide us,
Children of the flag are we.

# THE WASHERS OF THE SHROUD

## JAMES RUSSELL LOWELL

October 1861

\* \* \*

ALONG a riverside, I know not where,
I walked one night in mystery of dream;
A chill creeps curdling yet beneath my hair,
To think what chanced me by the pallid gleam
Of a moon-wraith that waned through haunted air.

Pale fireflies pulsed within the meadow-mist
Their halos, wavering thistledowns of light;
The loon, that seemed to mock some goblin tryst,
Laughed; and the echoes, huddling in affright,
Like Odin's hounds, fled baying down the night.

Then all was silent, till there smote my ear
A movement in the stream that checked my breath:
Was it the slow plash of a wading deer?
But something said, This water is of Death!
The Sisters wash a shroud, ill thing to hear!

I, looking then, beheld the ancient Three
Known to the Greek's and to the Northman's creed,
That sit in shadow of the mystic Tree,
Still crooning, as they weave their endless brede,
One song: Time was, Time is, and Time shall be.

No wrinkled crones were they, as I had deemed,
But fair as yesterday, to-day, to-morrow,
To mourner, lover, poet, ever seemed;
Something too high for joy, too deep for sorrow,
Thrilled in their tones, and from their faces gleamed.

"Still men and nations reap as they have strawn,"
So sang they, working at their task the while;
The fatal raiment must be cleansed ere dawn;
For Austria? Italy? the Sea-Queen's isle?
O'er what quenched grandeur must our shroud be drawn?

Or is it for a younger, fairer corse,
That gathered States for children round his knees,
That tamed the wave to be his posting-horse,
Feller of forests, linker of the seas,
Bridge-builder, hammerer, youngest son of Thor's?

What make we, murmur'st thou? and what are we?
When empires must be wound, we bring the shroud,
The time-old web of the implacable Three:
Is it too coarse for him, the young and proud?
Earth's mightiest deigned to wear it, why not he?

Is there no hope? I moaned, so strong, so fair!
Our Fowler whose proud bird would brook erewhile
No rival's swoop in all our western air!
Gather the ravens, then, in funeral file
For him, life's morn yet golden in his hair?

Leave me not hopeless, ye unpitying dames!
I see, half seeing. Tell me, ye who scanned
The stars, Earth's elders, still must noblest aims
    Be traced upon oblivious ocean-sands?
Must Hesper join the wailing ghosts of names?

When grass-blades stiffen with red battle-dew
Ye deem we choose the victor and the slain:
Say, choose we them that shall be leal and true
To the heart's longing, the high faith of brain?
    Yet there the victory lies, if ye but knew.

Three roots bear up Dominion: Knowledge, Will,
These twain are strong, but stronger yet the third,-
    Obedience, 'tis the great tap-root that still,
    Knit round the rock of Duty, is not stirred,
Though Heaven-loosed tempests spend their utmost skill.

Is the doom sealed for Hesper? 'Tis not we
Denounce it, but the Law before all time:
    The brave makes danger opportunity;
The waverer, paltering with the chance sublime,
    Dwarfs it to peril: which shall Hesper be?

Hath he let vultures climb his eagle's seat
To make Jove's bolts purveyors of their maw?
Hath he the Many's plaudits found more sweet
Than Wisdom? held Opinion's wind for Law?
    Then let him hearken for the doomster's feet.

Rough are the steps, slow-hewn in flintiest rock,
States climb to power by; slippery those with gold
    Down which they stumble to eternal mock:
No chafferer's hand shall long the sceptre hold,
Who, given a Fate to shape, would sell the block.

We sing old Sagas, songs of weal and woe,
Mystic because too cheaply understood;
Dark sayings are not ours; men hear and know,
See Evil weak, see strength alone in Good,
Yet hope to stem God's fire with walls of tow.

Time Was unlocks the riddle of Time Is,
That offers choice of glory or of gloom;
The solver makes Time Shall Be surely his.
But hasten, Sisters! for even now the tomb
Grates it's slow hinge and calls from the abyss.

But not for him, I cried, not yet for him,
Whose large horizon, westering, star by star
Wins from the void to where on Ocean's rim
The sunset shuts the world with golden bar,
Not yet his thews shall fail, his eye grow dim!

His shall be larger manhood, saved for those
That walk unblenching through the trial-fires;
Not suffering, but faint heart, is worst of woes,
And he no base-born son of craven sires,
Whose eye need blench confronted with his foes.

Tears may be ours, but proud, for those who win
Death's royal purple in the foeman's lines;
Peace, too, brings tears; and 'mid the battle-din,
The wiser ear some text of God divines,
For the sheathed blade may rust with darker sin.

God, give us peace! not such as lulls to sleep,
But sword on thigh, and brow with purpose knit!
And let our Ship of State to harbor sweep,
Her ports all up, her battle-lanterns lit,
And her leashed thunders gathering for their leap!

So cried I with clenched hands and passionate pain,
Thinking of dear ones by Potomac's side;
Again the loon laughed mocking, and again
The echoes bayed far down the night and died,
While waking I recalled my wandering brain.

# ANNAPOLIS

## WALDRON KINSOLVING POST

April, 1917 November, 1918

This tribute to the Naval Academy at Annapolis was written while the American squadron of destroyers was helping to preserve the freedom of the seas.

\* \* \*

THE mother sits by Severn side,
Where Severn joins the Bay,
And great gray ships go down the tide
And carry her sons away.
They carry them far, they carry them wide,
To all the Seven Seas,
But never beyond her love and pride,
And ever the deathless tales abide
They learned at the Mother's knees.

Stern she is, as well becomes
The nurse of gentle men,
Who trains their tread to roll of drums,
Their hands to sword and pen.

Her iron-blooded arteries hold
No soft Corinthian strain;
The Attic soul in a Spartan mould,
Loyal and hardy, clean and bold,
Shall govern the roaring main.

They come from South, they come from North,
They come from East and West;
And who can say, when all go forth,
That any of these are best?
With names unknown, and names that won
Their fame in a hundred fights,
The admiral's son, and the ploughman's son,
Mothered by her, they all are one,
Her race of sailor knights.

Young and eager and unafraid,
As neophytes they kneeled
And watched their arms, and only prayed
"Keep stain from every shield."
Naught else they fear as they hunt the foes
Through fog, and storm, and mine,
Keen for the joy of the battle blows;
But God make strong the hearts of those
Who love, and are left behind.

# MONTEREY

## CHARLES FENNO HOFFMAN

September 19th - 24th, 1846

The assaulting American army at the attack on Monterey
numbered six thousand six hundred and twenty-five; the
defeated Mexicans were about ten thousand.

\* \* \*

WE were not many we who stood
Before the iron sleet that day;
Yet many a gallant spirit would
Give half his years if but he could
Have with us been at Monterey.

Now here, now there, the shot it hailed
In deadly drifts of fiery spray,
Yet not a single soldier quailed
When wounded comrades round them wailed
Their dying shout at Monterey.

And on still on our column kept,
Through walls of flame, its withering way

Where fell the dead, the living stept,
Still charging on the guns which swept
　　The slippery streets of Monterey.

The foe himself recoiled aghast,
When, striking where he strongest lay,
We swooped his flanking batteries past,
And, braving full their murderous blast,
Stormed home the towers of Monterey.

Our banners on those turrets wave,
And there our evening bugles play;
Where orange-boughs above their grave
Keep green the memory of the brave
　　Who fought and fell at Monterey.

We are not many we who pressed
Beside the brave who fell that day;
But who of us has not confessed
He'd rather share their warrior rest
Than not have been at Monterey?

# THE REGULAR ARMY MAN

## JOSEPH C. LINCOLN

1898

\* \* \*

HE ain't no gold-laced "Belvidere,"
To sparkle in the sun;
He don't parade with gay cockade,
And posies in his gun;
He ain't no "pretty soldier boy,"

So lovely, spick and span,
He wears a crust of tan and dust,
The Regular Army man;
The marching, parching,
Pipe-clay starching,
Regular Army man.

He ain't at home in Sunday-school,
Nor yet a social tea,
And on the day he gets his pay
He's apt to spend it free;
He ain't no temperance advocate,

He likes to fill the can,
He's kind of rough, and, maybe, tough,
The Regular Army man;
The r'aring, tearing,
Sometimes swearing,
Regular Army man.

No State'll call him "noble son,"
He ain't no ladies' pet,
But, let a row start anyhow,
They'll send for him, you bet!
He don't cut any ice at all
In Fashion's social plan,-
He gets the job to face a mob,
The Regular Army man;
The milling, drilling,
Made for killing,
Regular Army man.

There ain't no tears shed over him
When he goes off to war,
He gets no speech nor prayerful preach
From mayor or governor;
He packs his little knapsack up
And trots off in the van,
To start the fight and start it right,
The Regular Army man;
The rattling, battling,
Colt or Gatling,
Regular Army man.

He makes no fuss about the job,
He don't talk big or brave,
He knows he's in to fight and win,
Or help fill up a grave;
He ain't no Mama's darling, but

He does the best he can,
And he's the chap that wins the scrap,
The Regular Army man;
The dandy, handy,
Cool and sandy,
Regular Army man.

# 44

# THE DYING VETERAN

## WALT WHITMAN

(A Long Island incident early part of the nineteenth century.)

* * *

AMID these days of order, ease, prosperity,
Amid the current songs of beauty, peace, decorum,
I cast a reminiscence
(likely it will offend you, I heard it in my boyhood)
More than a generation since,
A queer old savage man, a fighter under Washington
     himself
(Large, brave, cleanly, hot-blooded, no talker, rather
     spiritualistic,
Had fought in the ranks fought well had been
all through the Revolutionary war),
Lay dying sons, daughters, church-deacons, lovingly
     tending him,
Sharping their sense, their ears, towards his murmuring,
half-caught words:
"Let me return again to my war-days,
To the sights and scenes to forming the line of battle,
To the scouts ahead reconnoitering,

To the cannons, the grim artillery,
To the galloping aids, carrying orders,
To the wounded, the fallen, the heat, the suspense,
The perfume strong, the smoke, the deafening noise;
Away with your life of peace! your joys of peace!
Give me my old wild battle-life again!"

# 45

# ABRAHAM LINCOLN

## JAMES RUSSELL LOWELL

April 15th, 1865

This is a fragment of the noble Commemoration Ode delivered at Harvard College to the memory of those of its students who fell in the war which kept the country whole.

\* \* \*

SUCH was he, our Martyr-Chief,
Whom late the Nation he had led,
With ashes on her head,
Wept with the passion of an angry grief:
Forgive me, if from present things I turn
To speak what in my heart will beat and burn,
And hang my wreath on his world-honored urn.
Nature, they say, doth dote,
And cannot make a man
Save on some worn-out plan,
Repeating us by rote:
For him her Old World moulds aside she threw,
And, choosing sweet clay from the breast
Of the unexhausted West,

With stuff untainted shaped a hero new,
Wise, steadfast in the strength of God, and true.
How beautiful to see
Once more a shepherd of mankind indeed,
Who loved his charge, but never loved to lead;
One whose meek flock the people joyed to be,
Not lured by any cheat of birth,
But by his clear-grained human worth,
And brave old wisdom of sincerity!
They knew that outward grace is dust;
They could not choose but trust
In that sure-footed mind's unfaltering skill,
And supple-tempered will
That bent like perfect steel to spring again and thrust.
His was no lonely mountain-peak of mind,
Thrusting to thin air o'er our cloudy bars,
A sea-mark now, now lost in vapors blind,
Broad prairie rather, genial, level-lined,
Fruitful and friendly for all human kind,
Yet also nigh to heaven and loved of loftiest stars.
Nothing of Europe here,
Or, then, of Europe fronting morn ward still,
Ere any names of Serf and Peer
Could Nature's equal scheme deface;
Here was a type of the true elder race,
And one of Plutarch's men talked with us face to face.
I praise him not; it were too late;
And some innative weakness there must be
In him who condescends to victory
Such as the Present gives, and cannot wait,
Safe in himself as in a fate.
So always firmly he:
He knew to bide his time,
And can his fame abide,
Still patient in his simple faith sublime,
Till the wise years decide.

Great captains, with their guns and drums,
Disturb our judgment for the hour,
But at last silence comes;
These all are gone, and, standing like a tower,
Our children shall behold his fame,
The kindly-earnest, brave, foreseeing man,
Sagacious, patient, dreading praise, not blame,
New birth of our new soil, the first American.

# THE AMERICAN FLAG

## JOSEPH RODMAN DRAKE

May 29th, 1819

The penultimate quatrain [enclosed in brackets] ended the poem
as Drake wrote it, but Fitz Greene Halleck suggested the final
four lines, and Drake accepted his friend's quatrain in place of
his own.

\* \* \*

WHEN Freedom, from her mountain height,
Unfurled her standard to the air,
She tore the azure robe of night,
And set the stars of glory there!
She mingled with its gorgeous dyes
The milky baldric of the skies,
And striped its pure celestial white
With streakings of the morning light,
Then, from his mansion in the sun,
She called her eagle-bearer down,
And gave into his mighty hand
The symbol of her chosen land!

Majestic monarch of the cloud!
Who rear'st aloft thy regal form,
To hear the tempest-tramping loud,
And see the lightning-lances driven,
When stride the warriors of the storm,
And rolls the thunder-drum of heaven!

Child of the sun! to thee 'tis given
To guard the banner of the free,
To hover in the sulphur smoke,
To ward away the battle stroke,
And bid its blendings shine afar,
Like rainbows on the cloud of war,
The harbingers of victory!

Flag of the brave! thy folds shall fly,
The sign of hope and triumph high!
When speaks the signal-trumpet tone,
And the long line comes gleaming on,
(Ere yet the life-blood, warm and wet,
Has dimmed the glistening bayonet),
Each soldier's eye shall brightly turn
To where thy meteor-glories burn,
And, as his springing steps advance,
Catch war and vengeance from the glance!
And when the cannon-mouthings loud
Heave in wild wreaths the battle-shroud,
And gory sabres rise and fall,
Like shoots of flame on midnight's pall!
There shall thy victor-glances glow,
And cowering foes shall shrink beneath,
Each gallant arm that strikes below,
The lovely messenger of death.

Flag of the seas! on ocean's wave
Thy star shall glitter o'er the brave;

When Death, careering on the gale,
Sweeps darkly round the bellied sail,
And frighted waves rush wildly back
Before the broadside's reeling rack,
The dying wanderer of the sea
Shall look, at once, to heaven and thee,
And smile, to see thy splendors fly,
In triumph, o'er his closing eye.

Flag of the free heart's hope and home,
By angel hands to valor given!
Thy stars have lit the welkin dome,
And all thy hues were born in heaven!
[And fixed as yonder orb divine,
That saw thy bannered blaze unfurled,
Shall thy proud stars resplendent shine,
The guard and glory of the world.]
Forever float that standard sheet!
Where breathes the foe but falls before us?
With Freedom's soil beneath our feet,
And Freedom's banner streaming o'er us!

# 47

## BATTLE-HYMN OF THE REPUBLIC

### JULIA WARD HOWE

November, 1861

This war-song was written to the tune of "John Brown's Body," a tune to which many thousands of Volunteers were marching to the front.

\* \* \*

MINE eyes have seen the glory of the coming of the Lord:
He is trampling out the vintage where the grapes of wrath
    are stored;
He hath loosed the fateful lightning of His terrible swift
    sword:
His truth is marching on.

I have seen Him in the watch-fires of a hundred circling
    camps;
They have builded Him an altar in the evening dews and
    damps;
I can read His righteous sentence by the dim and flaring
    lamps.
His day is marching on.

I have read a fiery gospel, writ in burnished rows of steel:
As ye deal with My contemners, so with you My grace
    shall deal;
Let the Hero, born of woman, crush the serpent with His
    heel,
Since God is marching on.

He has sounded forth the trumpet that shall never call
    retreat;
He is sifting out the hearts of men before His judgment-
    seat:
Oh! be swift, my soul, to answer Him! be jubilant, my feet!
Our God is marching on.

In the beauty of the lilies Christ was born across the sea,
With a glory in His bosom that transfigures you and me:
As He died to make men holy, let us die to make men free.
While God is marching on.

# 48

# ANY WOMAN TO A SOLDIER

## GRACE ELLERY CHANNING

1917, 1918

\* \* \*

THE day you march away let the sun shine,
Let everything be blue and gold and fair,
Triumph of trumpets calling through bright air,
Flags slanting, flowers flaunting not a sign
    That the unbearable is now to bear,
    The day you march away.

The day you march away this I have sworn,
No matter what comes after, that shall be
Hid secretly between my soul and me
    As women hide the unborn
You shall see brows like banners, lips that frame
Smiles, for the pride those lips have in your name.
    You shall see soldiers in my eyes that day-
    That day, O soldier, when you march away.

The day you march away cannot I guess?
There will be ranks and ranks, all leading on

To one white face, and then the white face gone,
And nothing left but a gray emptiness-
Blurred moving masses, faceless, featureless-
The day you march away.

You cannot march away! However far,
Farther and faster still I shall have fled
Before you; and that moment when you land,
Voiceless, invisible, close at your hand
My heart shall smile, hearing the steady tread
Of your faith-keeping feet.

First at the trenches I shall be to greet;
There's not a watch I shall not share with you;
But more but most there where for you the red,
Drenched, dreadful, splendid, sacrificial field lifts up
Inflexible demand,
I will be there!

My hands shall hold the cup.
My hands beneath your head
Shall bear you not the stretcher bearer's through
All anguish of the dying and the dead;
With all your wounds I shall have ached and bled,
Waked, thirsted, starved, been fevered, gasped for breath,
Felt the death dew;
And you shall live, because my heart has said To Death
That Death itself shall have no part in you!

# 49

## AD FINEM FIDELES

### GUY WETMORE CARRYL

1898

This was written just after the end of the war with Spain for the freeing of Cuba.

\* \* \*

FAR out, far out they lie. Like stricken women weeping,
Eternal vigil keeping with slow and silent tread
Soft-shod as are the fairies, the winds patrol the prairies,
The sentinels of God about the pale and patient dead!
Above them, as they slumber in graves that none may
    number,
Dawns grow to day, days dim to dusk, and dusks in
    darkness pass;
Unheeded springs are born, unheeded summers brighten,
And winters wait to whiten the wilderness of grass.

Slow stride appointed years across their bivouac places,
With stern, devoted faces they lie, as when they lay,
In long battalions dreaming, till dawn, to eastward
    gleaming,

Awoke the clarion greeting of the bugles to the day.
The still and stealthy speeding of the pilgrim days
    unheeding,
At rest upon the roadway that their feet unfaltering trod,
The faithful unto death abide, with trust unshaken,
The morn when they shall waken to the reveille of God.

The faithful unto death! Their sleeping-places over
The torn and trampled clover to braver beauty blows;
Of all their grim campaigning no sight or sound
    remaining,
The memory of them mutely to greater glory grows.
Through waning ages winding, new inspiration finding,
Their creed of consecration like a silver ribbon runs,
Sole relic of the strife that woke the world to wonder
With riot and the thunder of a sundered people's guns.

What matters now the cause? As little children resting,
No more the battle breasting to the rumble of the drums,
Enlinked by duty's tether, the blue and gray together,
They wait the great hereafter when the last assembly
    comes.
Where'er the summons found them, whate'er the tie that
    bound them,
Tis this alone the record of the sleeping army saith:
They knew no creed but this, in duty not to falter,
With strength that naught could alter to be faithful unto
    death.

# WHEN THE GREAT GRAY SHIPS COME IN

## GUY WETMORE CARRYL

August 20, 1898

A week after the signing of the treaty of peace with Spain, Sampson's fleet came into New York harbor.

\* \* \*

TO eastward ringing, to westward winging, o'er mapless miles of sea,
On winds and tides the gospel rides that the further-most isles are free;
And the furthermost isles make answer, harbor, and height, and hill,
Breaker and beach cry, each to each, "Tis the Mother who calls! Be still!"
Mother! new-found, beloved, and strong to hold from harm,
Stretching to these across the seas the shield of her sovereign arm,
Who summoned the guns of her sailor sons, who bade her navies roam,

Who calls again to the leagues of main, and who calls
　　them this time home!

And the great gray ships are silent, and the weary
　　watchers rest;
The black cloud dies in the August skies, and deep in the
　　golden west

Invisible hands are limning a glory of crimson bars,
And far above is the wonder of a myriad wakened stars!
Peace! As the tidings silence the strenuous cannonade,
Peace at last! is the bugle-blast the length of the long
　　blockade;
And eyes of vigil weary are lit with the glad release,
From ship to ship and from lip to lip it is "Peace! Thank
　　God for peace!"

Ah, in the sweet hereafter Columbia still shall show
The sons of these who swept the seas how she bade them
　　rise and go;
How, when the stirring summons smote on her children's
　　ear,
South and North at the call stood forth, and the whole
　　land answered Here!
For the soul of the soldier's story and the heart of the
　　sailor's song
Are all of those who meet their foes as right should meet
　　with wrong,
Who fight their guns till the foeman runs, and then, on
　　the decks they trod,
Brave faces raise, and give the praise to the grace of their
　　country's God!

Yes, it is good to battle, and good to be strong and free,
To carry the hearts of a people to the uttermost ends of sea,

To see the day steal up the bay, where the enemy lies in
    wait,
To run your ship to the harbor's lip and sink her across
    the strait:

But better the golden evening when the ships round
    heads for home,
And the long gray miles slip swiftly past in a swirl of
    seething foam,
And the people wait at the haven's gate to greet the men
    who win!
Thank God for peace! Thank God for peace, when the
    great gray ships come in!

# SHERIDAN'S RIDE

## THOMAS BUCHANAN READ

October 19, 1864

General Early surprised and routed the Union troops during
General Sheridan's absence in Washington. Sheridan hastened
to the front, rallied his men, and won a complete victory.

\* \* \*

UP from the South at break of day,
Bringing to Winchester fresh dismay,
The affrighted air with a shudder bore,
Like a herald in haste, to the chieftain's door,
The terrible grumble, and rumble, and roar,
Telling the battle was on once more,
And Sheridan twenty miles away.
And wider still those billows of war
Thundered along the horizon's bar;

And louder yet into Winchester rolled
The roar of that red sea uncontrolled,
Making the blood of the listener cold,
As he thought of the stake in that fiery fray,

And Sheridan twenty miles away.
But there is a road from Winchester town,
A good, broad highway leading down;
And there, through the flush of the morning light,

A steed as black as the steeds of night,
Was seen to pass, as with eagle flight,
As if he knew the terrible need;
He stretched away with his utmost speed;
Hills rose and fell; but his heart was gay,
With Sheridan fifteen miles away.

Still sprung from those swift hoofs, thundering South,
The dust, like smoke from the cannon's mouth;
Or the trail of a comet, sweeping faster and faster,
Foreboding to traitors the doom of disaster.
The heart of the steed and the heart of the master
Were beating like prisoners assaulting their walls,
Impatient to be where the battle-field calls;
Every nerve of the charger was strained to full play,
With Sheridan only ten miles away.

Under his spurning feet the road
Like an arrowy Alpine river flowed,
And the landscape sped away behind
Like an ocean flying before the wind,
And the steed, like a bark fed with furnace fire,
Swept on, with his wild eye full of ire.
But lo ! he is nearing his heart's desire;
He is snuffing the smoke of the roaring fray,
With Sheridan only five miles away.

The first that the general saw were the groups
Of stragglers, and then the retreating troops,
What was done? what to do? a glance told him both,
Then striking his spurs, with a terrible oath,

He dashed down the line, mid a storm of huzzas,
And the wave of retreat checked its course there, because
The sight of the master compelled it to pause.
With foam and with dust, the black charger was gray
By the flash of his eye, and the red nostril's play,
He seemed to the whole great army to say,
"I have brought you Sheridan all the way
From Winchester, down to save the day!"

Hurrah! hurrah for Sheridan!
Hurrah! hurrah for horse and man!
And when their statues are placed on high,
Under the dome of the Union sky,
The American soldiers' Temple of Fame,
There with the glorious general's name
Be it said, in letters both bold and bright,
"Here is the steed that saved the day,
By carrying Sheridan into the fight,
From Winchester, twenty miles away!"

# FIFTY YEARS

## JAMES WELDON JOHNSON

1863 - 1913

On the Fiftieth Anniversary of the Signing of the Emancipation
Proclamation.

\* \* \*

O BROTHERS mine, to-day we stand
Where half a century sweeps our ken,
Since God, through Lincoln's ready hand,
Struck off our bonds and made us men.

Just fifty years a winter's day
As runs the history of a race;
Yet, as we look back o'er the way,
How distant seems our starting place!

Look farther back! Three centuries!
To where a naked, shivering score,
Snatched from their haunts across the seas,
Stood, wild-eyed, on Virginia's shore.

This land is ours by right of birth,
This land is ours by right of toil;
We helped to turn its virgin earth,
Our sweat is in its fruitful soil.

Where once the tangled forest stood,
Where flourished once rank weed and thorn,
Behold the path-traced, peaceful wood,
The cotton white, the yellow corn.

To gain these fruits that have been earned,
To hold these fields that have been won,
Our arms have strained, our backs have burned,
Bent bare beneath a ruthless sun.

That Banner which is now the type
Of victory on field and flood-
Remember, its first crimson stripe
Was dyed by Attucks' willing blood.

And never yet has come the cry
When that fair flag has been assailed
For men to do, for men to die,
That we have faltered or have failed.

We've helped to bear it, rent and torn,
Through many a hot-breath'd battle breeze;
Held in our hands, it has been borne
And planted far across the seas.

And never yet, O haughty Land,
Let us, at least, for this be praised
Has one black, treason-guided hand
Ever against that flag been raised.

Then should we speak but servile words,

Or shall we hang our heads in shame?
Stand back of new-come foreign hordes,
And fear our heritage to claim?

No! stand erect and without fear,
And for our foes let this suffice
We've bought a rightful sonship here,
And we have more than paid the price.

And yet, my brothers, well I know
The tethered feet, the pinioned wings,
The spirit bowed beneath the blow,
The heart grown faint from wounds and stings;

The staggering force of brutish might,
That strikes and leaves us stunned and dazed;
The long, vain waiting through the night
To hear some voice for justice raised.

Full well I know the hour when hope
Sinks dead, and 'round us everywhere
Hangs stifling darkness, and we grope
With hands uplifted in despair.

Courage! Look out, beyond, and see
The far horizon's beckoning span!
Faith in your God-known destiny!
We are a part of some great plan.

Because the tongues of Garrison
And Phillips now are cold in death,
Think you their work can be undone?
Or quenched the fires lit by their breath?

Think you that John Brown's spirit stops?
That Lovejoy was but idly slain?

Or do you think those precious drops
From Lincoln's heart were shed in vain?

That for which millions prayed and sighed,
That for which tens of thousands fought,
For which so many freely died,
God cannot let it come to naught.

# A TOAST TO OUR NATIVE LAND

## ROBERT BRIDGES

Paris, July 4, 1900

\* \* \*

HUGE and alert, irascible yet strong,
We make our fitful way 'mid right and wrong.
One time we pour out millions to be free,
Then rashly sweep an empire from the sea!
One time we strike the shackles from the slaves,
And then, quiescent, we are ruled by knaves.
Often we rudely break restraining bars,
And confidently reach out toward the stars.

Yet under all there flows a hidden stream
Sprung from the Rock of Freedom, the great dream
Of Washington and Franklin, men of old
Who knew that freedom is not bought with gold.
This is the Land we love, our heritage,
Strange mixture of the gross and fine, yet sage
And full of promise destined to be great.
Drink to Our Native Land! God Bless the State!

# THE CHOICE

## RUDYARD KIPLING

(THE AMERICAN SPIRIT SPEAKS)

April, 1917

\* \* \*

TO the Judge of Right and Wrong
I With Whom fulfillment lies
Our purpose and our power belong,
Our faith and sacrifice.

Let Freedom's Land rejoice!
Our ancient bonds are riven;
Once more to us the eternal choice
Of Good or ill is given.

Not at a little cost,
Hardly by prayer or tears,
Shall we recover the road we lost
In the drugged and doubting years.

But, after the fires and the wrath,

But, after searching and pain,
His Mercy opens us a path
To live with ourselves again.

In the Gates of Death rejoice!
We see and hold the good
Bear witness, Earth, we have made our choice
With Freedom's brotherhood!

Then praise the Lord Most High
Whose Strength hath saved us whole,
Who bade us choose that the Flesh should die
And not the living Soul!

To the God in Man displayed-
Where e'er we see that Birth,
Be love and understanding paid
As never yet on earth!

To the Spirit that moves in Man,
On Whom all worlds depend,
Be Glory since our world began
And service to the end!

# 55

# WITH THE TIDE

## EDITH WHARTON

January 6, 1919

This was written on the day after Theodore Roosevelt's death.

\* \* \*

SOMEWHERE I read, in an old book whose name
Is gone from me, I read that when the days
Of a man are counted, and his business done,
There comes up the shore at evening, with the tide,
To the place where he sits, a boat
And in the boat, from the place where he sits, he sees,
Dim in the dusk, dim and yet so familiar,
The faces of his friends long dead; and knows
They come for him, brought in upon the tide,
To take him where men go at set of day.
Then rising, with his hands in theirs, he goes
Between them his last steps, that are the first
Of the new life and with the ebb they pass,
Their shaken sail grown small upon the moon.

Often I thought of this, and pictured me

How many a man who lives with throngs about him,
Yet straining through the twilight for that boat
Shall scarce make out one figure in the stern,
And that so faint its features shall perplex him
With doubtful memories and his heart hang back.

But others, rising as they see the sail
Increase upon the sunset, hasten down,
Hands out and eyes elated; for they see
Head over head, crowding from bow to stern,
Repeopling their long loneliness with smiles,
The faces of their friends; and such go forth
Content upon the ebb tide, with safe hearts.

But never
To worker summoned when his day was done
Did mounting tide bring in such freight of friends
As stole to you up the white wintry shingle
That night while they that watched you thought you slept.
Softly they came, and beached the boat, and gathered
In the still cove under the icy stars,
Your last-born, and the dear loves of your heart,
And all men that have loved right more than ease,
And honor above honors: all who gave
Free-handed of their best for other men,
And thought their giving taking: they who knew
Man's natural state is effort, up and up-
All these were there, so great a company
Perchance you marvelled, wondering what great ship
Had brought that throng unnumbered to the cove
Where the boys used to beach their light canoe
After old happy picnics

But these, your friends and children, to whose hands
Committed, in the silent night you rose
And took your last faint steps

These led you down, O great American,
Down to the Winter night and the white beach,
And there you saw that the huge hull that waited
Was not as are the boats of the other dead,
Frail craft for a brief passage; no, for this
Was first of a long line of towering transports,
Storm-worn and ocean-weary every one,
The ships you launched, the ships you manned, the ships
That now, returning from their sacred quest
With the thrice-sacred burden of their dead,
Lay waiting there to take you forth with them,
Out with the ebb tide, on some farther quest.

# THE UNKNOWN SOLDIER

## ANGELA MORGAN

November 10, 1921

This poem was read by the author over the casket of the
Unknown Soldier, at the special memorial exercises held in the
rotunda of the Capitol at Washington.

\* \* \*

HE is known to the sun-white Majesties
Who stand at the gates of dawn.
He is known to the cloud-borne company
Whose souls but late have gone.
Like wind-flung stars through lattice bars
They throng to greet their own,
With voice of flame they sound his name
Who died to us unknown.

He is hailed by the time-crowned brotherhood,
By the Dauntless of Marathon,
By Raymond, Godfrey and Lion Heart
Whose dreams he carried on.
His name they call through the heavenly hall

Unheard by earthly ear,
He is claimed by the famed in Arcady
Who knew no title here.

Oh faint was the lamp of Sirius
And dim was the Milky Way.
Oh far was the floor of Paradise
From the soil where the soldier lay.
Oh chill and stark was the crimson dark
Where huddled men lay deep;
His comrades all denied his call-
Long had they lain in sleep.

Oh strange how the lamp of Sirius
Drops low to the dazzled eyes,
Oh strange how the steel-red battlefields
Are floors of Paradise.
Oh strange how the ground with never a sound
Swings open, tier on tier,
And standing there in the shining air
Are the friends he cherished here.

They are known to the sun-shod sentinels
Who circle the morning's door,
They are led by a cloud-bright company
Through paths unseen before.
Like blossoms blown, their souls have flown
Past war and reeking sod,
In the book unbound their names are found
They are known in the courts of God!

# READY

## PHOEBE CARY

1861

\* \* \*

LOADED with gallant soldiers,
A boat shot in to the land,
And lay at the right of Rodman's Point
With her keel upon the sand.

Lightly, gayly, they came to shore,
And never a man afraid;
When sudden the enemy opened fire
From his deadly ambuscade.

Each man fell flat on the bottom
Of the boat; and the captain said:
If we lie here, we all are captured,
And the first who moves is dead!

Then out spoke a negro sailor,
No slavish soul had he;
"Somebody's got to die, boys,

And it might as well be me!"

Firmly he rose, and fearlessly
Stepped out into the tide;
He pushed the vessel safely off,
Then fell across her side:

Fell, pierced by a dozen bullets,
As the boat swung clear and free;
But there wasn't a man of them that day
Who was fitter to die than he!

# YOU AND YOU

## EDITH WHARTON

### TO THE AMERICAN PRIVATE IN THE GREAT WAR

November, 1918

EVERY one of you won the war
You and you and you-
Each one knowing what it was for,
And what was his job to do.

Every one of you won the war,
Obedient, unwearied, unknown,
Dung in the trenches, drift on the shore,
Dust to the world's end blown;
Every one of you, steady and true,
You and you and you-
Down in the pit or up in the blue,
Whether you crawled or sailed or flew,
Whether your closest comrade knew
Or you bore the brunt alone

All of you, all of you, name after name,
Jones and Robinson, Smith and Brown,
You from the piping prairie town,
You from the Fundy fogs that came,

You from the city's roaring blocks,
You from the bleak New England rocks
With the shingled roof in the apple boughs,
You from the brown adobe house
You from the Rockies, you from the Coast,
You from the burning frontier-post
And you from the Klondyke's frozen flanks,
You from the cedar-swamps, you from the pine,
You from the cotton and you from the vine,
You from the rice and the sugar-brakes,
You from the Rivers and you from the Lakes,
You from the Creeks and you from the Licks
And you from the brown bayou
You and you and you
You from the pulpit, you from the mine,
You from the factories, you from the banks,
Closer and closer, ranks on ranks,
Airplanes and cannon, and rifles and tanks,
Smith and Robinson, Brown and Jones,
Ruddy faces or bleaching bones,
After the turmoil and blood and pain
Swinging home to the folks again
Or sleeping alone in the fine French rain
Every one of you won the war.

Every one of you won the war
You and you and you
Pressing and pouring forth, more and more,
Toiling and straining from shore to shore
To reach the flaming edge of the dark
Where man in his millions went up like a spark,

You, in your thousands and millions coming,
All the sea ploughed with you, all the air humming,
All the land loud with you,
All our hearts proud with you,
Ah l our souls bowed with the awe of your coming!

Where's the Arch high enough,
Lads, to receive you,
Where's the eye dry enough,
Dears, to perceive you,
When at last and at last in your glory you come,
Tramping home?

Every one of you won the war,
You and you and you
You that carry an unscathed head,
You that halt with a broken tread,
And oh, most of all, you Dead, you Dead!

Lift up the Gates for these that are last,
That are last in the great Procession.
Let the living pour in, take possession,
Flood back to the city, the ranch, the farm,
The church and the college and mill,
Back to the office, the store, the exchange,
Back to the wife with the babe on her arm,
Back to the mother that waits on the sill,
And the supper that's hot on the range.

And now, when the last of them all are by,
Be the Gates lifted up on high
To let those Others in,
Those Others, their brothers, that softly tread,
That come so thick, yet take no ground,
That are so many, yet make no sound,
Our Dead, our Dead, our Dead!

186

O silent and secretly-moving throng,
    In your fifty thousand strong,
Coming at dusk when the wreaths have dropt,
    And streets are empty, and music stopt,
        Silently coming to hearts that wait
        Dumb in the door and dumb at the gate,
        And hear your step and fly to your call-
            Every one of you won the war,
            But you, you Dead, most of all!

# TWILIGHT ON SUMTER

## RICHARD HENRY STODDARD

August 24, 1863

After the surrender of Major Anderson, the Confederates
strengthened the fort; but, in the spring of 1863, the U.S. guns
on Morris Island battered it into a shapeless ruin.

\* \* \*

STILL and dark along the sea
Sumter lay;
A light was overhead,
As from burning cities shed,
And the clouds were battle-red,
Far away.
Not a solitary gun
Left to tell the fort had won,
Or lost the day!
Nothing but the tattered rag
Of the drooping Rebel flag,
And the sea-birds screaming round it in their play.

How it woke one April morn,

Fame shall tell;
As from Moultrie, close at hand,
And the batteries on the land,
Round its faint but fearless band
Shot and shell
Raining hid the doubtful light;
But they fought the hopeless fight
Long and well,
(Theirs the glory, ours the shame!)
Till the walls were wrapt in flame,
Then their flag was proudly struck, and Sumter fell.

Now oh, look at Sumter now,
In the gloom!
Mark its scarred and shattered walls,
(Hark! the ruined rampart falls!)
There's a justice that appalls
In its doom;
For this blasted spot of earth
Where Rebellion had its birth
Is its tomb!
And when Sumter sinks at last
From the heavens, that shrink aghast,
Hell shall rise in grim derision and make room!

# THE MEN BEHIND THE GUNS

## JOHN JEROME ROONEY

1898

The high quality of American marksmanship was never more
conclusively shown than in the battle of Santiago.

\* \* \*

ACHEER and salute for the Admiral, and here's to the
Captain bold,
And never forget the Commodore's debt when the deeds
of might are told!
They stand to the deck through the battle's wreck
when the
great shells roar and screech
And never they fear when the foe is near to practice what
they preach:
But off with your hat and three times three for
Columbia's true-blue sons,
The men below who batter the foe the men behind the
guns!

Oh, light and merry of heart are they when they swing
    into port once more,
When, with more than enough of the "green backed stuff,"
they start for their leave-o'-shore;
And you'd think, perhaps, that the blue-bloused chaps
    who loll along the street
Are a tender bit, with salt on it, for some fierce
    "mustache" to eat
Some warrior bold, with straps of gold, who dazzles and
    fairly stuns
The modest worth of the sailor boys the lads who serve
    the guns.

But say not a word till the shot is heard that tells that the
    fight is on,
Till the long, deep roar grows more and more from the
    ships of "Yank" and "Don,"

Till over the deep the tempests sweep of fire and bursting
    shell,
And the very air is a mad Despair in the throes of a living
    hell;
Then down, deep down, in the mighty ship, unseen by the
    midday suns,
You'll find the chaps who are giving the raps the men behind
the guns!

Oh, well they know how the cyclones blow that they
    loose from their cloud of death,
And they know is heard the thunder-word their fierce
    ten-incher saith!
The steel decks rock with the lightning shock, and shake
    with the great recoil,
And the sea grows red with the blood of the dead and
    reaches for his spoil

But not till the foe has gone below or turns his prow and
    runs,
Shall the voice of peace bring sweet release to the men
    behind the guns!

# SHERMAN'S MARCH TO THE SEA

## SAMUEL H. M. BYERS

May 4th, 1864, December 21st 1864

After Sherman left Tennessee in May, to the taking of Atlanta
September 2nd, there was hardly a day without its battle; after
he left Atlanta he marched to the sea and took Savannah; then he
went to Columbia, and the backbone of the Rebellion was
broken. The poet wrote this while a prisoner at Columbia; and
when Sherman arrived there and read it, he attached Adjt. Byers
to his staff.

\* \* \*

OUR camp-fires shone bright on the mountain
That frowned on the river below,
As we stood by our guns in the morning,
And eagerly watched for the foe;
When a rider came out of the darkness
That hung over mountain and tree,
And shouted, "Boys, up and be ready!
For Sherman will march to the sea!"

Then cheer upon cheer for bold Sherman

Went up from each valley and glen,
And the bugles re-echoed the music
That came from the lips of the men;
For we knew that the stars in our banner
More bright in their splendor would be,
And that blessings from Northland would greet us,
When Sherman marched down to the sea.

Then forward, boys! forward to battle
We marched on our wearisome way,
We stormed the wild hills of Resaca
God bless those who fell on that day!
Then Kenesaw, dark in its glory,
Frowned down on the flag of the free;
But the East and the West bore our standard
And Sherman marched down to the sea.

Still onward we pressed, till our banners
Swept out from Atlanta's grim walls,
And the blood of the patriot dampened
The soil where the traitor-flag falls;
We paused not to weep for the fallen,
Who slept by each river and tree,
Yet we twined them a wreath of the laurel,
As Sherman marched down to the sea.

Oh, proud was our army that morning,
That stood where the pine darkly towers,
When Sherman said, "Boys, you are weary,
But to-day fair Savannah is ours!"
Then sang we the song of our chieftain,
That echoed o'er river and lea,
And the stars in our banner shone brighter
When Sherman marched down to the sea.

# YANKS

## JAMES W. FOLEY

1917-1918

\* \* \*

O'LEARY, from Chicago, and a first-class fightin' man,
For his father was from Kerry, where the gentle art began:
Sergeant Dennis P. O'Leary, from somewhere on Archie
    Road,
Dodgin' shells and smellin' powder while the battle ebbed
    and flowed.

And the captain says: "O'Leary, from your fightin'
    company
Pick a dozen fightin' Yankees and come skirmishin'
    with me;
Pick a dozen fightin' devils, and I know it's you who can."
And O'Leary, he saluted like a first-class fightin" man.

O'Leary's eye was piercin' and O'Leary's voice was clear:
"Dimitri Georgoupoulos!" And Dimitri answered "Here!"
Then "Vladimir Slaminsky! Step three paces to the front,
For we're wantin' you to join us in a little Heinie hunt!"

"Garibaldi Ravioli!" Garibaldi was to share;
And "Ole Axel Kettleson!" and "Thomas Scalp-the-Bear!"
Who was Choctaw by inheritance, bred in the blood and
    bones,
But set down in army records by the name of Thomas
    Jones.

"Van Winkle Schuyler Stuyvesant!" Van Winkle was a bud
From the ancient tree of Stuyvesant and had it in his
    blood;
"Don Miguel de Colombo!" Don Miguel's next of kin
Were across the Rio Grande when Don Miguel went in.

"Ulysses Grant O'Sheridan!" Ulysses' sire, you see,
Had been at Appomattox near the famous apple-tree;
And "Patrick Michael Casey!" Patrick Michael, you can
    tell,
Was a fightin' man by nature with three fightin' names as
    well.

"Joe Wheeler Lee!" And Joseph had a pair of fightin' eyes;
And his granddad was a Johnny, as perhaps you might
    surmise;
Then "Robert Bruce MacPherson!" And the Yankee squad
    was done
With "Isaac Abie Cohen!" once a lightweight champion.

Then O'Leary paced 'em. forward and, says he: "You
    Yanks, fall in!"
And he marched 'em to the captain. "Let the skirmishin'
    begin."
Says he, "The Yanks are comin', and you beat 'em if you
    can!"
And saluted like a soldier and first-class fightin man!

# THE BLUE AND THE GRAY

## FRANCIS MILES FINCH

1861 - 1865

The women of Columbus, Mississippi, had shown themselves
impartial in the offerings made to the memory of the dead. They
strewed flowers alike on the graves of the Confederate and of
the National soldiers.

BY the flow of the inland river,
Whence the fleets of iron have fled,
Where the blades of the grave-grass quiver,
Asleep on the ranks of the dead;
Under the sod and the dew,
Waiting the judgment day;
Under the one, the Blue;
Under the other, the Gray.

These in the robings of glory,
Those in the gloom of defeat;
All with the battle-blood gory,
In the dusk of eternity meet;

197

Under the sod and the dew,
Waiting the judgment day;
Under the laurel, the Blue;
Under the willow, the Gray.

From the silence of sorrowful hours,
The desolate mourners go,
Lovingly laden with flowers,
Alike for the friend and the foe;
Under the sod and the dew,
Waiting the judgment day;
Under the roses, the Blue;
Under the lilies, the Gray.

So, with an equal splendor,
The morning sun-rays fall,
With a touch impartially tender,
On the blossoms blooming for all;
Under the sod and the dew,
Waiting the judgment day;
Broidered with gold, the Blue;
Mellowed with gold, the Gray.

So, when the summer calleth,
On forest and field of grain,
With an equal murmur falleth
The cooling drip of the rain;
Under the sod and the dew,
Waiting the judgment day;
Wet with the rain, the Blue;
Wet with the rain, the Gray.

Sadly, but not with upbraiding,
The generous deed was done;
In the storm of the years that are fading,
No braver battle was won;

Under the sod and the dew,
Waiting the judgment day;
Under the blossoms, the Blue;
Under the garlands, the Gray.

No more shall the war-cry sever,
Or the winding rivers be red;
They banish our anger forever,
When they laurel the graves of our dead.
Under the sod and the dew,
Waiting the judgment day;
Love and tears for the Blue;
Tears and love for the Gray.

# 64

# I HAVE A RENDEZVOUS WITH DEATH

## ALAN SEEGER

1914, 1916

The writer of this was a member of the French Foreign Legion.
He was killed in action July 4, 1916.

\* \* \*

I HAVE a rendezvous with Death
At some disputed barricade,
When Spring comes back with rustling shade
And apple-blossoms fill the air
I have a rendezvous with Death
When Spring brings back blue days and fair.

It may be he shall take my hand
And lead me into his dark land
And close my eyes and quench my breath
It may be I shall pass him still.
I have a rendezvous with Death
On some scarred slope of battered hill,
When Spring comes round again this year
And the first meadow-flowers appear.

God knows 'twere better to be deep
Pillowed in silk and scented down,
Where Love throbs out in blissful sleep,
Pulse nigh to pulse, and breath to breath.,

Where hushed awakenings are dear.
But I've a rendezvous with Death
At midnight in some flaming town,
When Spring trips north again this year,
And I to my pledged word am true,
I shall not fail that rendezvous.

# 65

# AMERICA'S WELCOME HOME

## HENRY VAN DYKE

November 11, 1918

When the fighting ceased there were two million American soldiers in France.

\* \* \*

OH, gallantly they fared forth in khaki and in blue,
America's crusading host of warriors bold and true;
They battled for the rights of man beside our brave Allies,
And now they're coming home to us with glory in their
eyes.

Oh, it's home again, and home again, America for me!
Our hearts are turning home again and there we long
to be,
In our beautiful big country beyond the ocean bars,
Where the air is full of sunlight and the flag is full of stars.

Our boys have seen the Old World as none have seen
before.
They know the grisly horror of the German gods of war:

The noble faith of Britain and the hero-heart of France,
The soul of Belgium's fortitude and Italy's romance.

They bore our country's great word across the rolling sea,
"America swears brotherhood with all the just and free."
They wrote that word victorious on fields of mortal
strife,
And many a valiant lad was proud to seal it with his life.

Oh, welcome home in Heaven's peace, dear spirits of the
dead!
And welcome home ye living sons America hath bred!
The lords of war are beaten down, your glorious task is
done;
You fought to make the whole world free, and the
victory is
won.

Now it's home again, and home again, our hearts are
turning west,
Of all the lands beneath the sun America is best.
We're going home to our own folks, beyond the ocean
bars,
Where the air is full of sunlight and the flag is full of stars.

# 66

# GROVER CLEVELAND

## JOEL BENTON

1837 - 1908

On June 24, 1908, Grover Cleveland, twice President of the United States, died at his home in Princeton, N. J., at the age of seventy-one.

\* \* \*

BRING cypress, rosemary and rue
For him who kept his rudder true;
Who held to right the people's will,
And for whose foes we love him still.

A man of Plutarch's marble mould,
Of virtues strong and manifold,
Who spurned the incense of the hour,
And made the nation's weal his dower.

His sturdy, rugged sense of right
Put selfish purpose out of sight;
Slowly he thought, but long and well,
With temper imperturbable.

Bring cypress, rosemary and rue
For him who kept his rudder true;
Who went at dawn to that high star
Where Washington and Lincoln are.

# THE BURIAL OF SHERMAN

## RICHARD WATSON GILDER

1820, 1891

Sherman died on January 14. His funeral took place two days later. The statue by Saint Gaudens was unveiled in NewYork in 1903.

\* \* \*

GLORY and honor and fame and everlasting laudation
For our captains who loved not war, but fought for
the life of the nation;
Who knew that, in all the land, one slave meant strife, not
peace;
Who fought for freedom, not glory; made war that war
might cease.

Glory and honor and fame; the beating of muffled drums;
The wailing funeral dirge, as the flag-wrapt coffin comes.
Fame and honor and glory, and joy for a noble soul;
For a full and splendid life, and laurelled rest at the goal.

Glory and honor and fame; the pomp that a soldier
    prizes;
The league-long waving line as the marching falls and
    rises;
Rumbling of caissons and guns; the clatter of horses' feet,
And a million awe-struck faces far down the waiting
    street.

But better than martial woe, and the pageant of civic
    sorrow;
Better than praise of to-day, or the statue we build to-
    morrow;
Better than honor and glory, and History's iron pen,
Was the thought of duty done and the love of his
    fellow-men.

6 8

# THE AMERICAN VOLUNTEERS

## MARIE VAN VORST

August, 1914 April, 1917

In the long months before the United States entered the war
many Americans took service under the flag of France.

\* \* \*

NEUTRAL! America, you cannot give
To your sons' souls neutrality. Your powers
Are sovereign, Mother, but past histories live
In hearts as young as ours.

We who are free disdain oppression, lust
And infamous raid. We have been pioneers
For freedom and our code of honor must
Dry and not startle tears.

We've read of Lafayette, who came to give
His youth, with his companions and their powers,
To help the Colonies and heroes live
In hearts as young as ours!

Neutral! We who go forth with sword and lance,
A little band to swell the battle's flow,
Go willingly, to pay again to France
Some of the debt we owe.

# THE UNKNOWN SOLDIER

## HENRY WADSWORTH LONGFELLOW

\* \* \*

Thou, too, sail on, Ship of State!
Sail on, Union, strong and great!
Humanity, with all its fears,
With all the hopes of future years,
Is hanging breathless on thy fate!
We know what Master laid thy keel,
What Workmen wrought thy ribs of steely
Who made each mast, and sail, and rope,
What anvils rang, what hammers beat,
In what a forge and what a heat
We're shaped by the anchors of thy hope!
Fear not each sudden sound and shock
'Tis of the wave and not the rock,
'Tis but the flapping of the sail,
And not a rent made by the gale!
In spite of rock and tempest's roar,
In spite of false lights on the shore,
Sail on, nor fear to breast the sea!

Our hearts, our hopes, are all with thee,
Our hearts, our hopes, our prayers, our tears,
Our faith triumphant o'er our fears,
Are all with thee, are all with thee.

34204452R00130